PARTY STUDIES

VOLUME 2

Party Studies

VOLUME 2

Underground clubs, parallel structures and second cultures

edited: VÍCTOR AGUADO
RAMÓN DEL BUEY
BRANDON LABELLE

ERRANT BODIES PRESS, BERLIN
AMEE, MADRID

as part of Communities in Movement: research on social acoustics, escape, and common life

CONTENT

Introduction: partying from below

VÍCTOR AGUADO, RAMÓN DEL BUEY,
BRANDON LABELLE

Since the publication of volume 1 in the Party Studies series, we've continued to elaborate the concept through conversations and workshops, as well as creative activity in different contexts. We've been greatly encouraged by the positive responses and shared interests expressed by friends and colleagues, as well as new and emerging collaborations. The topic of party studies in general sparks a lot of joy and curiosity, and it's this affectionate sharing that feels supportive, in terms of *keeping things going*. Following the first volume, which brought focus to the topic of house parties, and how domestic environments and living spaces afford important opportunities for gathering together, we've been led to consider the relation between parties and secrecy. Part of what emerged in the first volume was recognizing the aspect of secrecy, withdrawal, a *being-hidden* that often pervades house parties – in withdrawing to the home, parties become private affairs and gain a certain social charge, in which ducking under or gathering outside official sites contributes to the exuberance and meaningfulness of being together. Yet, this privateness or secrecy is equally giving way to a new form of publicness or communal power: to withdraw, to be secret, or to gather in the home environment of others, invites a new sense of potentiality for what we may do together both inside and outside the home. This is part of the political potency always embedded in the house party, and parties more generally.

Extending from volume 1, this second volume concentrates on the question of secrecy more directly. In what ways does secrecy and being-hidden participate in shaping parties and the drive or necessity of alternative communal life? How to negotiate the challenges around visibility and invisibility, especially in contexts shaped by fear and vulnerability? How do notions of the underground operate as a key imaginary for subcultural expression? Is clandestinity, and gestures of exit, necessary for working against a given social order?

It is our interest to reflect upon secrecy and parties, and how the clandestine qualities of underground cultures for example become both necessary and rich in cultural meaning. Identities and communities may in fact gain potency through participating in something secret, hidden, withdrawn: there is a certain *underground imagination* at play, one which persists, shaping the primary myth of *partying from below*. Such mythologies though are fully grounded in real life situations, in which withdrawal and staying below may be vital to survival and being safe. It may also provide opportunities for playing out alternative rhythms, ways of inhabiting environments, of creating something special outside dominant systems and sites. These are perspectives reflected upon throughout volume 2 of Party Studies.

Questions of secrecy find a particular expression in the essay by Nina Dragičević. Looking into the history of queer spaces, particularly those of lesbian bars, Dragičević examines the ways in which sound and music operate to enable communicating queer desire. This includes appreciating how such communications must often contend with dominant heteronormative codes as well as cultures of homophobia at times pervading bar environments. Charting the lesbian scene within Ljubljana in particular, Dragičević offers important insight into how secrecy enables protection while also maintaining and celebrating forms of queer life through surprising loudness.

Dragičević's essay opens key aspects of parties, where the joy of being together must at times negotiate a complex politics of identity and place, fear and vulnerability. These concerns are further articulated in the contribution by artist Nayara Leite. Based on a performance work presented in Bergen, Norway, in 2021, Leite draws attention to LGBTQ+ communities in their home country of Brazil, and how these communities struggle against pervasive homophobia and violence. In particular, Leite tells the story of Casa Nem, a LGBTQ+ shelter and sanctuary based in Rio de Janeiro. Since 2016 Casa Nem has provided much needed support for queer and trans persons, acting as a safe space as well as unique home in which to live and thrive. Leite's performative work, developed in collaboration with Kiyoshi Yamamoto, presents both a celebration as well as a call for greater recognition; drawing upon carnival traditions from Brazil, her contribution brings the party into the open, asking audiences to join in honoring the diverse forms love may take.

Moving from issues of queer love, and the ways in which secrecy is navigated in protecting as well as celebrating togetherness, secrecy is given further reflection and manifestation in the work of Adam Kraft. An artist based in Berlin, Kraft works at occupying buildings and sites in the city, often giving way to creative forms of breaking and entering, key duplication, tunneling and critical acts of invisibility. Through a conversation with editor Brandon LaBelle, Kraft describes the An-Akademie, a secret academy occupying a site in central Berlin since 2019. The An-Akademie provides a compelling articulation of underground approaches, where being invisible opens a new social imaginary for how the city can be bent, reshaped, made otherwise – especially in terms of giving time and space for nurturing forms of praxis together.

Breaking in, ducking under, hiding out, these are ways of reclaiming a right to the city that do not necessarily demand entry into the arena of public culture. Rather, they are driven by a belief in the power of secrecy, of exit, of partying from below, as what can support creative living and community. To party from below is positioned as a parallel polis which, as Brandon LaBelle maps in his article, speaks toward a general form of resistance. Bringing forward an autobiographical story of teenage life, LaBelle elaborates an understanding of secrecy that equally addresses survival and protection; it also opens toward conceptualizing the hidden as what aims at upsetting dominant mechanics of oppositional politics. To exit may also be about creating parallel structures and second cultures, terms which take guidance from the Prague underground from the 1970s and 80s.

Between autobiography and fiction there is no distinction that operates as an either/or polarity, as there is no such distinction between the overt and the hidden, brightness and darkness, openness and secrecy. Common to all of them, however, is that they are figurative operations. The mimesis in every autobiographical story assumed operative is one mode of figuration among others. The found handwritten stories by Mauro Benavidez figure three different Latin American soundsystem party scenes – Colombian *picó*, Mexican *sonidero*, and Brazilian *aparelhagem*. They happen in the street, sometimes in full sight, but operate in codes that are almost incomprehensible to any outsider. First, the *picó* is huge and itinerant, travelling the roads of the Atlantic coast of Colombia like a mobile totem. Its loudspeakers spread the Afro-Caribbean rhythms of champeta. They are decorated with an iconography that represents worship motifs, and some people dedicate a lifetime to owning them. Three illustrations by Dairo E. Barriosnuevo-Marín were found together with the first handwritten story, and are included here too. The Mexican *sonido* also comes and goes. It can emerge in bustling markets, such as Tepito, where the crowd dances to the rhythm of cumbia, salsa and guaracha announced by the voice of Lupita La Cigarrita, as is the case in the second scene described. During these parties, requests to her are spread out in a frenzied rush, amplified frantically by the microphone as the crowd swirls in a hedge of loudspeakers bordering it. The *aparelhagem* of Belém, another bordering area, is steeped in the local imaginary. The legends of the territory and the dj booth take the form of exuberantly living creatures, such as the jaguar, the wolf, the crocodile or the pink dolphin, which appear and disappear to hunt, regurgitate or reproduce. The sonorous vitality of this mysterious, voluptuous and wild beast can engulf dancing bodies on the outskirts of cities near the mouth of the Amazon.

One can read these tales while listening to the songs that *picotero* Don Alirio has selected and mixed for this volume (this session, called *Una fiesta eterna*, is available on the Errant Bodies website), for which, moreover, editors Víctor Aguado and Ramón del Buey write an essay on Le Larraskito Kluba – an important space in Bilbao, Basque Country, which hosted underground experimental music parties from 2008 – 2020. The documentary material that remains of Larraskito club is very fragile, because it is the document of a moment. Every possibility of publication, of extending its life beyond this moment, would be incoherent. All that remains are some DIY photographs, some audio and video recordings, and the ephemera that accompanied the events that were convened clandestinely – materials which were not thought to be history, and were at times best suited to disappear. However, some of those ephemera appear in these pages.

One of Larraskito's purposes was to transform the rowdy atmosphere of Bilbao's musical counterculture into another political and festive environment, but one that was compatible with less exuberant sensibilities and ways of living together, such as practices of attentive listening or the organization of conviviality based on mutual support. In relation to this affective mutation, Lucía Jalón considers clandestinity as a demand for sensorial acuity, production of space and reserve beyond the scope of a logic of domination. It is a creative approach, according to which secrecy is an agency and goes beyond opposition or resistance to the cultural history of diurnalization, whose epicenter we can locate in the hegemonic countries of Europe during the 17th and 18th centuries, with events such as the expansion of the normalized State, the legal regulation of the night or the birth of the public lighting system and the modern police force. The production of a clandestine spatiality is not understood in terms of the construction of a closed form, a zone of darkness or a problem of visibility, but, in a Spinozian line of thought, as a balance of powers that must be reconfigured at every moment. Hence the interest in studying the party without resorting to counterpositions with the dominant political paradigm, nor making completely explicit what it hides.

The potentiality of bypassing dichotomous or oppositional configurations between above and below, apparent and hidden, finds a parallel in the article by curator Dayang Yraola. Bringing into focus the social phenomenon tambay in the context of the Philippines, Yraola captures a more nuanced form of partying, where the emergent act of hanging out with others is less about clandestinity; rather, tambay figures a communal gathering that appears without clear boundaries or temporalities, and that no less supplies an important social energy to the delimitations of daily life. As Yraola suggests, the unpurposeness of tambay, and the ways in which community and connection may be fostered by way of its attitude, is suggestive for approaching parties less as institutionalized and even recognizable forms, and more as ambiguous and highly potent improvisations.

It is this tension between transparency and opacity that marks the party, reminding us that every party is itself full of multiple parties, where secret gestures are passed behind the back or in corners that enable the hatching of plans.

BAR

BAR

Meet Me Halfway – Sound, Music, and the Disco Club in Construction of Lesbian Communities

NINA DRAGIČEVIĆ

Sound moves. But not only in itself. The mere presence of sound has the capacity not only to move objects – but also to construct moving subjects. And a moving subject is a necessary condition for an active, vital, emancipatory political organism. So we go.

It was Sunday, more than a decade ago. While the majority of the population prepares for the forthcoming week, the homosexuals of Ljubljana hit the clubs. A club, Klub K4 – a nightclub that was and still is known for regularly hosting a so-called *Roza disko* (Pink Disco), a disco night produced by and for homosexuals, transgender people, and other persons of non-normative sexual and gender identities. I entered. There was who appeared to be a woman DJ spinning electronic music, a sort of *techno*. All around the dance floor, there were glorious, though seemingly bored-out-of-their-minds, lesbians. Some stood still by the bar, some leaned on the walls. Okay, I thought to myself, so this is the lesbian scene.

A week later, I repeat my visit to the club. Everything is the same, yet everything is different. The club was now bursting at the seams, dwelling in the vocal flow of an ex-Yugoslav singer Lepa Brena – and so were the lesbians. They, who a week ago

This text is based on, with parts translated from, the book *Med njima je glasba: Glasba v konstrukciji lezbične scene* by Nina Dragičević (2017).

would by no means take their hands out of their pockets and thus threaten their cool, their stoic yet very telling posture, now had their hands just below the ceiling, waving them around, dancing with each other, touching each other as, via the speakers, another ex-Yugoslav singer, Neda Ukraden, was singing *da se nađemo na pola puta*, meaning *meet me halfway*.

Again, everything was the same – geographically and architecturally unchanged space, more or less the same clientele, the same kind of drinks, no sudden changes in terms of reaching equal rights for homosexual people. But something was different. The sonic composition of the space. The music. What thus activated this line of thought is that the spatial sonic composition might be crucial for the dynamics on a lesbian scene, as well as for its very construction.

Why would a lesbian scene be interesting for observation in this regard? What is it that makes it so vibrant, so exciting? Flirtation. A lesbian scene is out-and-out satured with flirtation. Flirtation is the drive and the reason for the existance of a lesbian scene in the first place. A place for flirting which may continue both into physicality and sexuality and towards creative and political action. Flirtation is so nuclear to a lesbian scene that there its members are sometimes allowed behaviors that would be marked as inappropriate in environments with more conservative sexual morals. But not on the lesbian scene, as there, in its essence, there are no traditional patriarchal (gender-) power relations that would make one or the other a priori subordinate. The basic drive is mutual, that is, *lesbian* desire.

One of the main techniques through which the lesbians in Ljubljana first started getting together in a semi-organized, informal way was by placing anonymous magazine adverts.[1] But these were precarious events and they took place out in the open, not in a safe space. The lesbians needed a space where their processes of connecting, bonding, flirting, seducing, executing their lesbian desires and the necessity of political activation could be carried out both in a safe environment and, which is equally important, in a continuous, non-precarious manner. Such a place is a lesbian nightclub.

The frontal stimuli in any nightclub are sounds; they mostly take place in the form of what is usually – although not without its problems – called music. Music is at the forefront of a situation of the lesbian process of seduction which through multiplication in a space *defined* by a specific sonority is the becoming of a lesbian scene with the potential of becoming a community. But how is this process carried out? How do we arrive from an occurrence of a person somewhere and another elsewhere to an occurrence of a lesbian scene, a group of lesbians in a space that is inhabited by them continuously? I propose to look for the answer to that question in the construction of a lesbian. Here, I am somewhat pointing to the writings of philosopher Teresa de Lauretis and one of her major points: "it takes two women, not one, to make a lesbian."[2] What constitutes them as lesbian subjects is a shared fantasy, a lesbian fantasy. A certain contact is necessary. What sonority and music have to do with that can be sketched out through an example which can be found in a book by Elizabeth Lapovsky Kennedy and Madeline Davis, *Boots of leather, slippers of gold*, in which the authors studied the formations of early lesbian scenes in the United States in the 1940s, in an era of extreme explicit homophobic policies and likewise extreme everyday homophobia.

The lesbian scenes, as spaces outside private environments, in the US, as well as in Europe, started to develop mainly

1 A case from August 1984 shows a weekly magazine publish a letter from Roni who invites the readers "similar to me" to join her in a park to hang out, as she "can't seem to find the right crowd" in which she could feel "at ease". She ends her invitation with: "I hope I don't end up sitting there alone." See Greif and Velikonja, *Lezbična sekcija LL: kronologija 1987-2012 s predzgodovino*. Ljubljana: ŠKUC, p. 59.

2 Lauretis. 1994. *The Practice of Love: Lesbian Sexuality and Perverse Desire*. Bloomington and Indianapolis: Indiana University Press. p. 92.

through the lesbians populating various bars which were at first dominated by the heterosexual population. Lesbians got to know each other there, and through their contacts, flirtations, friendships, and relationships they also developed distinct lesbian genders, such as butch and fem. Here is how this initial process, taking place in a public space, a bar, is described in *Boots of leather, slippers of gold*:

> After seeing someone she is attracted to, the first thing the fem would do is ask someone she already knew the name of her chosen butch and her status: 'Is she going with anybody?' If she found that the butch might be available, a fem might get up from her seat and go to the jukebox, making sure she crossed the butch's line of vision as closely as she could manage. She would spend quite some time staring at the title listing (even if she knew it by heart already!) and occasionally glancing in the butch's direction. She would then manage to play a song that might directly indicate her interest.[3]

A situation of becoming lesbian. And more, a specific communication, a situation of a specific bond being knit. And yet, none of the interlocutors have spoken a word. A certain affection and attraction are being expressed, and it can be communicated without words because there is music between them. However, what is central to this event is not merely an act of expression but a practice of *listening*. Not a practice of hearing the unavoidable atmospheric sonority or furniture music, but a precisely directed attention + interpretation. Most importantly: what is being observed, listened to, has broader social consequences.

Of course, not speaking is in no way an outstanding achievement. However, as a rule, the beginnings of lesbian scenes and communities take place in the social sphere of homophobia, and being outspoken in such a sphere is not an obvious, let alone a safe step. And yet there is desire which wishes to step out of the sphere of fantasy and enter into the space of possible realization, a space in which an individual will have the necessary conditions for subjectivization beyond the historical social norm, that is, as a lesbian. Sound compositions and their dynamics play a crucial role in the creation of such conditions. They also make available the emancipatory effects, such that subvert an individual alienation into a potential for a societal, cultural, and political community.

When there was a lack of original music tracks by (known, outed) lesbians which would explicitly thematize lesbian desire, the lesbians listened to dominantly heterosexual narratives. There was the popular music, the musicians such as Perry Como, Buddy Holly, Elvis Presley, Frank Sinatra, all those authors who expressed potency and vitalism as a social – and strictly male-centered, patriarchal – ideal. They often applied a discursive subversion to these songs – just as with other elements of identity performance, they appropriated the songs so that they communicated their *lesbian* desire. Lesbian singers Lisa Ben and Beverly Shaw, for example, change the lyrics of the song *Hello, Young Lovers* from the Rodgers and Hammerstein musical, *The King and I*, a song later recorded by Sinatra and Como: what was once "I've had a love like you," is now substituted with "I've had a butch like you."[4] They *lesbianize* it. In the late 1940s, Lisa Ben – an acronym for 'lesbian' – is also an editor of one of the earliest American homophile magazines. She dedicates an entire section of the paper to Lyricature, a subversion of popular songs. There, we also find, for example, an appropriation of the Leo Robin's in Richard A. Whiting's 1930s hit song *My Ideal*:

3 Lapovsky Kennedy and Davis. 1994. "Boots of Leather, Slippers of Gold: The History of a Lesbian Community". Middlesex, Penguin. p. 239.

4 Faderman. 1992. *Odd girls and twilight lovers: a history of lesbian life in twentieth-century America*. New York: Penguin. p. 221.

Will I ever find A girl of my kind A girl who's a Mate to me?	⟶	*Will I ever find A girl of my kind A girl who's a Mate to me?*
Maybe she's a dream And yet she might be just around the corner looking for me,	⟶	*Maybe she's afraid To make up her mind. If she only would, tho, I know she'd find Someone who'd adore Her ever more and more And nothing from her conceal.*
Or will I pass her [him] by And never even know that	⟶	*Where ever she may stay My sad heart longs there to be gay*
She [he] was my ideal?		*With My Ideal.*

My Ideal was recorded by many authors, first Maurice Chevalier and Sam Lanin's Famous Players in 1930, in the next decade by Maxine Sullivan and Jimmy Dorsey, and then by Dinah Washington, Chet Baker, and Pearl Bailey – the latter also performed with the comedian, singer, and lesbian, Jackie 'Moms' Mabley, but in all the recordings, the gender of 'the ideal' provides a heterosexual narrative. Laurajean, the author at Vice Versa, on the other hand, appropriates it into the lesbian narrative. Her sad heart wants to be joyful (gay) with *her*.

In the winter edition of the magazine, Laurajean continues. This time, there is no possibility for any misunderstanding as to her argument. She even adds her own lyrics. This time, she treats a Billboard no. 1 track, The Andrews Sisters' *Near You*:

There's just one place for me,	⟶	*There's just one way for me:*
near you		*GAY WAY!*
It's like heaven to be,		*It's my nature to be*
near you		*GAY WAY!*
/		*'Boy meets girls meets heart'*
		I don't consider smart.
		Butch meets fluff--that's luff!'
		Is my idea of hot stuff!
If my hours could be spent	⟶	*If my hours could be spent*
near you		*GAY WAY,*
I'd be more than content		*I'd be "jammed" if I went*
near you		*A-WAY!*
Make my life worthwhile		*Never'd be a square,*
By telling me that I'll		*Not even on a dare.*
spend the rest of my days		*Want to live all my life*
near you		*GAY WAY!*

A similar, though distinct process was made by Marlene Dietrich on the song *My Baby Just Cares for Me*. She does not change the narrative of a song, she keeps the pronouns intact, but this song was mainly sung by male singers (Bing Crosby, James Dean, etc.) and the lyrics presented the 'Baby' as a woman. (When Nina Simone performed the song, the pronoun changed to 'he' to preserve the heterosexual narrative.) Her version was recorded in 1961 so she does add some then-popular names into the lyrics, but as the narrative is not changed to normatively suit her gender, it is precisely because of that changed in a non-normative, i.e. lesbian one. Dietrich who is *perceived to be a woman* sings:

My baby's no Como fan
and Elvis is not her man
my baby just cares for me
My baby don't care for Marlon Brando
she'd rather have me to hold her hand, oh ...

There are so many cases of *such a queering the song*, as Anno Mungen terms it.[5] Central to them is that through the morphological appropriation of the songs on their lyrical and musical levels as well as the popular singers' representation narratives the lesbian listener was (and is) in a position to discursively demolish the dominant norms of gender and sexuality representations and, by linking their performative practices with their sexual difference, they were (and are) in a position to create new, i.e. lesbian genders and cultures. By such an appropriation, they did (and do) the same to the dominant sonorities.

The fem arrives at the jukebox. She picks a song. She does not choose just any song. Because she wants to communicate a specific kind of interest to the other one, it seems reasonable to assume that she chooses a song which within the established discourses of articulation and interpretation of romantic and/or erotic desire will communicate just that. She inscribes her romantic and/or sexual desires for the other into the song. The heterosexual narrative is thus appropriated by a lesbian one. When they listen to this song separately, in solitude (which may as well occur in a public space), their desire exists only in the form of a fantasy; it does not yet imply the possibility of realization; they imagine a utopia. Fantasy may seem like an alternative that would be better than reality – in both personal and political terms – but is not yet historically possible. However, when they meet, for example by the jukebox where one selects a song to address the other, a fantasy can materialize in the form of a possibility of realization. Crucially: they need not say a word.

The fem chooses, for example, Elvis Presley's *Can't help falling in love*. It is a song she[6] had probably listened to before, she knows the song and has thought about a potential lover who sings to her saying that *only fools rush in*, but she really *can't help falling in love with* her. But this works in two distinct ways. The "butch" is now placed in a position of a listener who is at once also in a position of the messenger: she can be the one who sings to her potential lover (via the singer on the record), for she is the one whose sources for the performance of her lesbian gender are both the image and the sound techniques of the singer (Elvis Presley) as well as the song itself. One person approaches the other by the jukebox. Elvis Presley fills the space – the *public* space – with a specific sonically, rhythmically, and verbally expressed

5 Cf. Mungen, Anno. 2011. "Anders als die Anderen," or Queering the Song: Construction and Representation of Homosexuality in German Cabaret Song Recordings before 1933. *Queering the Popular Pitch*, ed. Sheila Whiteley in Jennifer Rycenga, 67-80. New York and London: Routledge. Mungen shows us a case of the artist Paul O'Montis singing the song *Was hast du Gefühle, Moritz?* The song speaks about Moritz, a man who is somehow unsure of who to love and who to be; he likes both men and women. The transition between different desires and feelings or the duality of desire is clearly articulated by the performer in the absence of a visible body (only his voice coming from the record) through the manipulation of his voice – radical changes in pitch, singing 'low', then singing 'high' – which can be understood as articulating the transitions between gender and sexual identities.

6 I want to be very clear with my choice of the pronoun for our "fem", as well as our "butch" personas. Not only are we here analyzing an example from a book that deals with lesbian societal groupations in the 1940s when the modern concepts, such as cis-gender, were not in use, I am also not implying that by terming the "fem" a "she" is to presume that the fem's identity is in fit with her assigned sex and/or her gender expression. Quite the contrary, I use this pronoun to state that the "fem" is merely likely to be *perceived as* a "she" (as a social category of 'woman') by the (patriarchal) social system, no matter what her subjective identity is. Furthermore, in an instance of *lesbian genders*, I follow Monique Wittig's materialist feminist line of thought in which a lesbian can by definition not be a woman because the occurrence of 'woman' takes place only in a relation, not as an individual or autonomous phenomenon; a lesbian is not a woman and not a man, but "has to be", as Wittig would put it, "a something else, a not-woman, a not-man". (Wittig, *The Straight Mind And Other Essays*, 1992, Boston, Beacon Press, p. 13) However, a "fem" is, to emphasize again, likely to be perceived as a woman.

sentimentality. The "butch", who in this event approaches the "fem" who selected precisely *this* song precisely *for her*, now, precisely because of the communicative mediator which is music, de facto steps out of the closet as a new subject, she approaches her as a lesbian.

In this process, the sonority (both atmospheric-social and musical-cultural) of a space manages to create what we might term a *bidirectional sonic desire transfer*. By this I mean a transcription of an image of a subject that the other is observing into a consumed sonic composition, and her transfer into the same composition, as well as the inverse process, the transcription of the consumed sonic composition into the person which the composition is interpellating.

It might seem that the emancipatory potential of sound (in this case, music) is delivered entirely in a one-on-one relation. However, I suggest we notice that once a specific sonority has communicated the erotic, sexual, sentimental interest, we have in front of us the first lesbian bond (connection) – and each that follows is a cornerstone of a lesbian scene which is a starting point for a community.

The fact that the lesbian cultures often relied on the appropriation and subversion of heterosexual narratives in popular music is not to say that there was an absolute lack of lesbians composing and producing music, attempting on singer-songwriter careers, and in other musical genres. From Francesca Caccini's operatic compositions to Lucille Bogan, Gertrude Ma Rainey, Chavela Vargas, Alberta Hunter, and Gladys Bentley to the artists under the Olivia Records umbrella and numerous other lesbian-feminist record labels of the second wave feminism as well as the musicians who did not get their chance within any of the larger lesbian-feminist record labels, such as Kathy Fire and Maxine/Max Feldman, to name only a few who worked in the same geopolitical area as our jukebox case, there have always been lesbian authors who explicitly expressed a lesbian desire in their artistic performances. But while the areas such as North America have a long tradition of lesbian singer-songwriters and musicians, a different case is to be made when we fast-forward a few decades and several thousand kilometers to the "lesbian Ljubljana".

In terms of the dynamics of sound and the developments of lesbian scenes and communities, the ones in Ljubljana are marked with historical specifics. If many, if not most, historical lesbian scenes are in at least some regard marked with singers-songwriters, the one in Ljubljana structured itself around a lesbian DJ who, strictly speaking, through her own lesbian desire and ability to fulfill very specific (and constitutive) music requests, played a kind of a role of a jukebox we spoke about earlier, and vice versa, the lesbian DJ could and did only constitute herself as such within a lesbian scene and/or community. The lesbian community in Ljubljana has produced an impressive number of DJs. It should go without saying that this was only possible once the infrastructural problems (i.e. lack of space for continuous encounters) were solved. In 1993, at the height of the new civil-society movements which started in the 1980s, several groups of artists and activists squatted the former military buildings of Metelkova – a neighborhood in the very center of Ljubljana – and later on turned them into nightclubs, concert venues, and artist studios. One of the buildings was squatted by a group of gay and lesbian individuals. Soon enough, this empty building was turned into the gay nightclub, Tiffany, and the lesbian nightclub, Monokel, both of which have become two of the main nightlife venues in Ljubljana.

Club Monokel has always been not only a nightclub but also a lesbian bar and cultural venue. Among its various programmatic elements, there were also DJ workshops for women and lesbians, and the DJ booth was pretty much open to anyone of the lesbian scene's members. It thus comes to no surprise that the musical genres played in Monokel had a rather broad horizon – as the DJs took their turns, one could hear everything from jazz to bhangra to punk to pop to techno to drum'n'bass to house to breakbeat to ska to partisan songs and the so-called "Balkan Music". The letter might be of higher concern, especially regarding the 1990s, as it shows an interesting case of identity salience. While Slovenia had already declared its independence and the remains of Yugoslavia were falling apart via the war in Bosnia and Herzegovina, Croatia, and Serbia, leaving thousands of refugees fleeing the war through Slovenia or staying within its borders, this was still a mutual cultural space. The analysis of music being listened to in Monokel in the 90s shows how the mediatory force of music in the construction of lesbian scenes and sexual identity sometimes manages to completely overshadow even the most problematic political stances of the artist-singer. In 90s Monokel we can on some occasions hear music from several musicians who took explicit Ustaš or Četnik political stands during the war. But their political stands seem to have been entirely irrelevant in the community (or at least in a segment of this community) that was tightly connected to the then-new progressive civil society movements. This topic could and should be further explored, but it reaches outside the scope of this text. We may, for now, say that the music by the so-called Yugoslav artists had an enormous impact on the construction of the lesbian scene and that the main purpose of most of the music played in a lesbian nightclub was to somehow express the erotic or the romantic; not just through lyrics but also specific melodic and rhythmic structures. Such are the popular songs that echo the point made on the case of Elvis Presley's *Can't help falling in love*. Take, for example, Neda Ukraden's *Da se nađemo na pola puta* (en. *Meet Me Halfway*). The singer expresses an explicit heterosexual narration, she

addresses “her man”, speaks about “his pride” which prevents him from making a crucial step in their relationship, so she proposes to meet somewhere in the middle. But she only expresses precisely this narrative if the listener accepts a listening position that reproduces precisely this narrative. What wishes to be said is now being said by this song.

Or take another example, the songs by Zdravko Čolić, a singer with a kind of an 80s superstar status in Yugoslavia. One of his most popular songs played in Monokel was *Pusti pusti modu* (album Zbog tebe, 1980) The lyrics of this song could be criticized from a feminist stand at nearly any verse. He sees the person (woman) in question as a *little doll from Trieste*, she is the object of observation. But again, everything changes when we specify the listener and the space – at least two lesbians in a lesbian club. As a pair who is outside a man-woman relation, they cease to be women, they become lesbians and it becomes possible for them to inhabit lesbian genders. Their listening takes place in a lesbian space where they are surrounded by other lesbians, i.e. in a space of mutual (lesbian) fantasy where this fantasy holds an ambition to be realized. This fantasy is now being mediated without their vocal utterances but by the music as a sonic transfer mode of the message.

While some popular songs certainly mark homosexual social spaces, they do not enter spontaneously, just as these social spaces do not occur out of nowhere. It is first the construction of these spaces as sonic spaces that allows for their musical and sonic development. While they appear to be spheres of fun, laughter, and entertainment, it is necessary to understand these spaces as spheres of serious social critique and even defiance. When a subordinate and/or a marginal social group is exposed to destruction, often even before it has managed to present itself as a group, when destruction does not take place on an explicit materialized level, when it is somewhere in the air, spreading through it and seeping through every crack, when it appears that no escape is available, when the surrounding society seems to be receptive to, and participates in, the invisible forces of destruction, what can a marginalized and repressed group and more specifically a homosexual group do if it wants to fight these maneuvers of repression, these often intangible and ubiquitous tendencies to marginalize and destroy? They are to create a disco club.

Homosexual disco club as an activator of a movement. A space that becomes a homosexual disco club when homosexuality settles and voices it. Not in any way, but loudly. So loudly that an individual has to strain if they want to communicate verbally, and even then they only contribute to this very loudness. A nightclub is a space of sociality in which loud sonority is at its forefront. The club is only established on the grounds of loud sonority – it is this that makes a nightclub a nightclub. The sonority that establishes it is not in no way random but rather a materialized effect of a certain ideological, discursive design. While sounds are always present in society, they are defined both through their object of origin and the listening position. In their representation as loud, they are often an explicit declaration of power, they can be a means of terror, dehumanization, and annihilation. However, they can also be used as means for an act against oppression. When an oppressed group uses loud sounds precisely to confront and resist the loudness and omnipresence of the oppressor and its dominant sonorities, in other words, when an oppressed group realizes that sounds are not a given but are produced from a vital organism which then uses precisely sounds to renew its vitality, the effect of loud sonority can have a subversive effect. What seemed to be inaudible becomes more audible and this audibility replaces, even expels other audibilities, the general and dominant and repressive become *the other*, the sonorities of homosexuality are now in the foreground, this sonic construction is now the music of homosexuality, it is loud and frontal, it dictates the dynamics in this space. The individual, the lesbian in a homosexual nightclub then does not observe her sexual difference but listens to sexual familiarity, if not sameness.[7]

The music of homosexuality is constructed from both what is conventionally termed music and the seemingly spontaneous vocal and atmospheric utterances of the inhabitants of this space, and this construction is a crucial building block of homosexuality and homosexual scenes as plateaus of designing and performing sexual difference and sexual sameness, romantic links, as well as political action. The loudness which nowadays seems to be a matter of irritation here presents itself as potentially emancipatory. It is delivered in most part by the DJ who in a homosexual, or even lesbian club is often a DJ who is also a lesbian or is *perceived as* such. The DJ implies a position of power. She 'loudly' communicates and dictates the dynamics in the space of her auditory authority. The music spun by the DJ in a homosexual or lesbian disco club (or any other nightclub for that matter) can be understood as an authoritarian force that asserts and renews its position, firstly, through an amplitude greater than the volume of individual sounds, a kind of forcefulness with a potential for territorialization, and secondly, it provides comfort and security by creating conjunction out of individual bodies.

In the club, the authority of sound is determined and it plays its role actively. In that sense, it's not that *tonight god is a DJ*, as the hit club song would say, but quite the reverse, the DJ is now acting as god. Beyond the submissiveness to which they have been subjected, for the people on the dance floor, the club's sound construction is a platform on which one can relieve their subjective social body from the imperative of docility, moderation, and specific historical norms, even if only for a short time. But the effects might be long-term. In close proximity to others, these bodies are in a position to recognize and experiment with sexuality and the erotic. They can attempt to articulate that which until then only lived in a semi-lingual fantasy as a framework of desire. To be sure, these processes are in no way autonomous, there is no authenticity, as these bodies are not only social bodies but are conducting subjectivation in the construction of and within a specific sonically constructed space. Furthermore, despite relevant criticisms of the culture industry as one that depoliticizes or obscures the critical social perspective through pleasure and entertainment, for the homosexual, in our case lesbian population, a disco club can be put into the category of critical infrastructure.

Lesbian individuals need spaces for their encounters to even become lesbians. At the same time, their social reality is that of omnipresent homophobia, making any explicit verbal articulation of their sexual desire always in danger of being sanctioned. No matter how progressive and liberal any society may declare itself to be, coming out always was and still is a brave action. A necessary one, but also a brave one. Coming out is for an individual not a one-time event, it happens every single day. While the task of the lesbian DJ is to constantly renew the materialized environment in which lesbian desire wishes to enter, the presence of each person on the dance floor is not only put in relation with others and not only with the DJ, but also with the walls of the space that they grind and reshape over and over again with their backs, palms, the soles of the shoes they lean on when performing a stoic cool posture or are kissing their lover. The frictions that are created by making the walls subject to the bass lines of that night's hits, the vibrations of bodies (not just any bodies), and the cultural symbolism of the space, contribute to the sonic creation of a lesbian territory. The rhythmicity of the vibrations, whether it's a metronomically precise DJ set, rubbing of elbows by the bar,

7 Sameness should not be mistaken for universality.

or the make-out (anti)patterns there in the corner, the continuance of the rhythmic and sonic social gestures into an illusion of harmony is a lesbian space. But spaces, perhaps especially lesbian spaces, need to be occupied over and over again to preserve themselves. Every Friday night with lesbians in a lesbian space that can't be lesbian without them is not a logical, self-evident event, it is each time an occupation of space. Furthermore, a disco club by and for homosexuals, by and for lesbians, allows for not only a coming out via the music as a mediator but serves also as a complex mechanism for the qualitative articulation of the subjectivity that is now out or on its way there. Not only does the population of a homosexual nightclub dwell in its sound structure, it concurrently creates it. The disco club *is its sonic structure*. The process of its creation is not and can not be static. Each sonic utterance, be it verbal, physical, or musical, adds to the structure which is a sonic composition, thereby constantly changing it.

The very songs spun by the lesbian DJ who, this needs to be emphasized, again and again, is in tremendous control of the club's sound sphere because she 1) is in control of amplitude and this also affects the amplitude of the population, and 2) appears as a possible representation of 'lesbian' and thus serves as a point of identification – her music selection inhabits the space between the social bodies in the club. There, music can serve as a mediator and a connector, as a communicator which expresses that which is not being said but is perhaps thought. This is not to say that the bodies on the dancefloor or by the bar are silent. Rather, they are now in a position to expand their mechanisms of expression (via gaze, facial expression, body movement, etc.), all of which constructively complicates and develops language. At least two persons are there, the music is between them, it suggests for them to meet halfway. Once they do, we are presented with lesbians, which is to say we are presented with a departure from a social norm, which is to say we are presented with their future experience of social response to this departure, which is to say we are presented with a certain antagonism, a conflict, which is to say we are presented with a possibility of a political movement. The disco club had to be a disco club.

KIM
KIM

I decided to share my love with you

INTRODUCTION

NAYARA LEITE

I came across Casa Nem sometime in 2020. A former professor had emailed me suggesting that I should watch the documentary *Indianara*, as it would be relevant for my research about the LGBTQ+ community in Brazil. The documentary brings forward the powerful trajectory of Casa Nem's founder Indianarae (previously called Indianara) Siqueira, a trans activist that dedicates her life to fight for the survival of those within this community.

The first major project that Indianarae conceived was Prepara Nem, a course that prepares all LGBTQ+ people – although it gives priority to *travestis*[1] and transgender women – to enter the university. Volunteers give their time to teach the ones who can't have access to education, either for financial reasons or because they don't feel safe in other classrooms. A year later, in 2016, Indianarae noticed how some of the students were having housing problems, such as living in shelters in risky conditions or suffering violence from their families. That realization made her expand Prepara Nem and create Casa Nem, an LGBTQ+ sanctuary in Rio de Janeiro. Casa Nem is not only a shelter, but a safe-space for those struggling to live in a supportive environment because of their sexuality and gender identity.

After being expelled – not always peacefully – from the different houses where Casa Nem tried to make its headquarters, Indianarae and Casa Nem's inhabitants fought hard to have a

1 travesti – originally a pejorative term, it has been reappropriated in the past few years by Brazilian, Peruvian and Argentinians activists. In these countries, travestis are recognized as a non-binary and political identity.

permanent space. And they got it. In 2020, they moved to a house of their own in the Flamengo neighborhood. It's there where 50 vulnerable LGBTQ+ people found a family and a roof over their heads. Prepara Nem is now hosted at Casa Nem's new location, and so are many workshops, which are giving them opportunities to find jobs and live a more dignified life.

However, Casa Nem doesn't receive any help from Brazil's current government. And with a self-proclaimed homophobic president, the fight has become even harder. So, they depend on the donations they get, and every month they share, through their social media channels, a list with the basic items they need to keep the house functioning. In a country where the life expectancy of a trans person is 35-years old, having a place like Casa Nem brings a little hope to this community.

In the end of 2020, I was invited by Norwegian artist and curator Maya Økland to work on a performance in collaboration with fellow Brazilian artist Kiyoshi Yamamoto. The performance would be part of one of the events related to the unveiling of the sculpture entitled *Benkene til Kim* (Kim's benches), which is dedicated to Norwegian gay rights activist Kim Friele (1935–2021). The sculpture, made by artist Lina Viste Grønli would be the first one for *Kvinner på sokkel* (Women on plinths), a 10-year project developed by the Bergen municipality, in which they'd erect five sculptures of significant women in the city.

In our many meetings to brainstorm and discuss our collaboration, Kiyoshi and I agreed right from the start that we wanted to give something back to our home country. When I mentioned that we should raise funds to Casa Nem – the organization was still fresh in my mind as I had just watched the documentary – Kiyoshi promptly said yes. Coming from Rio, he had already heard about Casa Nem. We wanted to support Casa Nem as a place where LGBTQ+ people find much needed sanctuary, and where relationships amongst the community can be nurtured outside of heteronormativity. Such safe-spaces become essential for those marginalized by the larger society, allowing for personal identities and the making of extended families to thrive. In this regard, the environment of Casa Nem contributes to empowering the LGBTQ+ community, which includes the need to fortify and protect against discrimination and violence. So, we joined forces: Kiyoshi made the costumes and masks; I wrote the text for the performance and made the layout for the posters.

On the opening of Bergen Pride, in June 2021, we presented "I decided to share my love with you" for the first time. The performance took shape as a small-scaled carnivalesque parade in the city center, finally arriving at *Benkene til Kim*, where a prepared text was read aloud accompanied by drumming. The text speaks about what it means to have privileges, and included a harsh criticism of president Jair Bolsonaro's dangerous government during the pandemic, as well as a shopping list poem inspired by Casa Nem's latest list with the basic items they need. The performance also included drums and colorful costumes inspired by the *Maracatu*[2] tradition of the state of Pernambuco. At the end of the reading, the participants of the performance – which included Kiyoshi and me – left the benches and walked back to the starting point of the parade. We stopped midway and revealed to the audience the back of our costumes, which also functioned as signage spelling out the word PRIVILEGE.

Throughout the whole week after the performance, we hosted an online auction where the masks made by Kiyoshi were sold. Posters and t-shirts were also sold during and after Pride Week. In the end, all the money we raised from selling these pieces went directly to Casa Nem. It's the least we could do to help an

2 Maracatu is an Afro-Brazilian folklore manifestation practiced in the states of Pernambuco and Ceará. There are different kinds of Maracatu, and Maracatu Nação is the one that gave inspiration to our performance. The origin of Maracatu Nação comes from the coronation ceremonies of the Reis do Congo (Kings of Congo), who were slaves with leadership roles within the slave community during Colonial Brazil. When slavery was abolished in 1888, the ceremony continued to exist and is now performed during the Carnival holiday.

organization that has been surviving and thriving through one of the darkest times that our home country has been facing. It's us looking at our own privileges, acknowledging them, and hopefully making people think about their own privileges as well.

HAVE YOU THOUGHT ABOUT YOUR PRIVILEGES TODAY?

TEXT BY NAYARA LEITE

Have you thought about your privileges today?
The privilege of being white in a racist society.
Where the color of your skin doesn't determine the amount of fear you feel when the police are approaching with their guns, with their power.
Where you can
breathe.

Have you thought about your privileges today?
The privilege of being male in a misogynistic society.
Where you can wear whatever you want without being harassed, without being raped.
Where you can walk alone at night
fearless.

Have you thought about your privileges today?
The privilege of being rich in an elitist society.
Where you don't have to decide if this month you'll be able to buy either medicine or butter or deodorant.
Where the money for your rent will never be a
struggle.

Have you thought about your privileges today?
The privilege of being straight in a homophobic society.
Where you don't have to let the hand of your partner go when walking on the street.
Where the person you love doesn't need to be a
secret.

Have you thought about your privileges today?
The privilege of being cisgender in a transphobic society.
Where your gender identity won't be the reason for you to be unemployed or the reason to have your life shortened.
Where you know you'll come back home
alive.

Have you thought about your privileges today?
The privilege of living in a country where the government treats a pandemic with seriousness.
Where the government doesn't lie about the side effects of the vaccine by saying that men's voices will turn "effeminate".
Where the government doesn't encourage people to wear masks by saying that doing so is "too gay".
Where the government doesn't tell its citizens to stop dealing with the pandemic like a "country of fags".
Where the government doesn't use defamatory language in regards to an already neglected community.
Where the government actually cares.
What a privilege it is
to live in a country like
this.

[pause]

Casa Nem is a non-profit organization that shelters queer and trans people in Rio de Janeiro.
Casa Nem doesn't receive any support from Bolsonaro's government.

Casa Nem needs
Sugar

Casa Nem needs
Salt

Casa Nem needs
Black beans

Casa Nem needs
Rice

Casa Nem needs
Oil

Casa Nem needs
Vinegar

Casa Nem needs
Olives

Casa Nem needs
Olive oil

Casa Nem needs
Eggs

Casa Nem needs
Mozzarella

Casa Nem needs
Pasta

Casa Nem needs
Tomato paste

Casa Nem needs
Flour

Casa Nem needs
Milk cream

Casa Nem needs
Corn for popcorn

Casa Nem needs
Coconut milk

Casa Nem needs
Vegetables

Casa Nem needs
Fruits

Casa Nem needs
Milk

Casa Nem needs
Yeast

Casa Nem needs
Canned corn

Casa Nem needs
Canned peas

Casa Nem needs
Onion

Casa Nem needs
Garlic

Casa Nem needs
Spices

Casa Nem needs
Grated cheese

Casa Nem needs
Chocolate powder

Casa Nem needs
Sauces

Casa Nem needs
Gelatine

Casa Nem needs
Coffee

Casa Nem needs
Juice

Casa Nem needs
Tea

Casa Nem needs
Butter

Casa Nem needs
Mayonnaise

Casa Nem needs
Cake dough

Casa Nem needs
Bread

Casa Nem needs
Cookies

Casa Nem needs
Shaver

Casa Nem needs
Make up

Casa Nem needs
Deodorant

Casa Nem needs
Toothbrushes

Casa Nem needs
Shampoo

Casa Nem needs
Conditioner

Casa Nem needs
Disinfectant

Casa Nem needs
Bleach

Casa Nem needs
Soap bar

Casa Nem needs
Washing powder

Casa Nem needs
Insecticides

Casa Nem needs
Detergent

Casa Nem needs
Chlorine

Casa Nem needs
Rubbish bags

Casa Nem needs
Sponges

Casa Nem needs
Broom

Casa Nem needs
Squeegee

Casa Nem needs
Dustpan

Casa Nem needs
Dog food

Casa Nem needs
Cat food

Casa Nem needs
Cat litter box

ALLERIET

HOTEL BERGEN BØRS

Die Schule

An-Akademie – demanding the impossible

ADAM KRAFT

Imagine yourself in front of a framed picture on the wall. Nothing spectacular. But when you pull the frame gently, the picture snaps out of place and effortlessly swings open, offering a passage for you to enter. Once inside this chamber, you push open a second door and step into a dimly lit room, the air smells of coffee and ink.

You can still hear the roar from the street; cars and buses, the chiming of church bells, distant chatter. But you're out of sight, even when you drop the curtains to let the daylight in.

A spacious hall built from red-brown bricks is revealed before you, with islands of bricolaged furniture spread across the space – a small library, a printing press, benches, tables, screens, a kitchen on wheels. Before you know it, you're joined by others.

Welcome to the An-Akademie!

Fig.1. Amidst the rambling in the framed testimony there's a valid point – "The proximity to the Praxis was and will remain a specialty." The An-Akademie is a clandestine space for studies, where praxis is promoted as primary. You can access it through a number of hidden passageways. This is one of them.

BRANDON LABELLE: Your work is mostly based on acts of trespassing, entering into hidden spaces or interstitial cavities that are off-limits within the urban fabric. What led you to this approach as an artist?

ADAM KRAFT: To begin with I'm kind of uneasy with the label of 'work' and of 'being an artist.' Not only does it presuppose a kind of disciplinization of identity, but it also immediately places you within a logic and a rationality of labor. Positioning individuals within a landscape of capitalism, what you 'do for a living'. Indirectly, I guess this answers your question regarding acts of trespassing. I'm interested in putting reasoning into praxis, into acts of transgression that refuses and challenges the rationality of the hegemony; the urban neoliberal fabric and its deadening effect on everyday life, through processes of gentrification, social centrifugation, displacement, austerity, gig-employments, and with widening social gaps as one of many alarming consequences. Add to that its suffocating machinery that seamlessly transforms critical culture into instruments in the branding of the "creative city". Altogether, this creates a setting of monolithic urbanism – a capitalist realism where the current condition is promoted as the only alternative.

So, with acts of transgression – or trespassing as you refer to it – there's an effort in transforming the city into a permeable structure. In that sense, the interstitial cavity appears closely related to what Ernst Bloch referred to as the *utopian margins*, something that Avery F. Gordon has researched and developed further. The utopian margins, as Gordon argues, has its historical roots in slaves running away, marronage, piracy, heresy, witchcraft, vagrancy, vagabondage, rebellion, soldier desertion, and other often illegible, illegitimate, or trivialized forms of escape, resistance, opposition, and alternative ways of life (Gordon).

Fig.2. For the past couple of decades the site was managed by a group of investors to simulate a four-floor edifice. A top-to-bottom fake façade banner was wrapped around a scaffolding. As this was dismantled by the authorities I repurposed the material into screens for projections and partitions. Curtains were cut from the same stock. When hauled down, the pompous architecture surrounding the An-Akademie is unveiled while the school space remains concealed.

In spatial terms Gordon describes it as an elusive, vague and secretive place that emerges and recedes in practical relationships with others. A *Temporary Autonomous Zone* of sorts, or a Pirate Utopia, to hinge it with the philosophical legacy of Hakim Bey.

> LABELLE: From what I know of your work or praxis, you often develop activities alone, or with a single collaborator. Though your interventions are also often an invitation to unknown others, to make hidden or locked spaces accessible, and to follow your tracks so to speak. This seems to shift with the An-Akademie project in Berlin, where you explicitly open a space for many others to join and to use the space for their interests and activities. Can you say something about this, how is this happening? Do you feel this is a collaborative process, a way of building a kind of secret community?

KRAFT: Well, the praxis I'm involved in is very process driven. It's also relational, in one way or another, as it deals with public space and conditions for social imagination. The collaborative formula differs depending on the conditions; whether spatial or cultural. With the An-Akademie the possibilities for social participation increased thanks to the sizable dimensions of the space.

Let me give you some background information to make the narrative about the An-Akademie a bit more comprehensible. After the wall came down in Berlin, with all its voided venues in combination with a raging city revitalization plan, there were a bunch of Potemkin façades erected around town. Most of which were initiatives from private lobby groups to render public desire for the reconstruction of past edifices. 1:1 full scale façades, printed on tarpaulin and wrapped around gigantic webs of scaffolding. There were three really big ones; one replicating The Berlin Palace at the museum island (installed 1994), one at

Potsdamer Platz (installed 2001) and one at Schinkel Platz, replicating the Bauakademie (installed 2004). I found these baumaske[1] incredibly powerful. Not the façades as such, but the unplanned bewilderment that sprouted behind them, the interstitial topography of a nature turned inside out. But as real-estate capital ballooned, one after the other fake façade was replaced with blustery construction sites and was eventually transformed into brick-and-mortared apparitions of its dead past. The once utopian margins ended up buried under monoliths of capital, concrete and retrotopianism.

The last one existing of these unruly hinterlands was the old Bauakademie, facing the ministry of foreign affairs. Here, I ended up secretly squatting a shack at the top of the scaffolding. I completely rebuilt the interior, fitting it as a space for small social gatherings. Contesting the idea of an academy it was offered as an underground study space. Hinging on the historical past of the place and space, I named it the An-Bau. *An-* as an anarchist adaptation of anarchitecture, understood as an autonomous social practice fusing art and science where buildings, rooms and other bodies are out of control. *Bau* (German for building; structure; construction) relating to the conservative and retrofuturist concept of the Building Academy; a higher education relating to architecture, construction and urban development.

In November 2016 the Berlin Bundestag released €62m to finance the reconstruction. Exactly three years later the scaffolding and its fitted plastic façade was deinstalled. Consequently, that was the end of the An-Bau study space. The only thing left standing on site was the showroom of the Bauakademie, where the planning and lobbying meetings had been held, now left deserted. A window was left unlocked and so the subsequent was initiated, the An-Akademie.

1 Baumaske; a Building Mask, a definition that was established in German after these façades had been erected. It's the representation of the storey, eaves and ridge height of a planned building on a scale of 1:1 on its building site, in order to visualize the dimensions of this building at site during the planning phase.

INTERNATIONALE BAUAKADEMIE BERLIN

Fig.3. View of scaffolding and facade with appropriated shack – the An-Bau.
Photo by Mischa Leinkauf.

LABELLE: As an academy, the An-Akademie is also posing a certain relation to knowledge, or practices of knowledge production, which I find interesting. What kinds of practices and discourses are happening there? Do you feel the An-Akademie makes an intervention not only onto the architecture, but also onto approaches to knowledge?

KRAFT: I would say that the An-Akademie ticks the box of a utopian margin; an underground autonomous space for social experimental praxis. Claiming that space and place – with its history of knowledge production and its recent ongoing plans of once again becoming an academy relating to architecture and urban development – involves contesting past, present and future ideas of urbanism. The core study within the An-A involves questions on autonomy, emancipation and radical imagination, and how these can be put into practice. Here, the setting and situation is understood to affect the outcome. A situated and situationed imagination if you wish. On the one hand, imagination is stimulated by the seemingly impossible setting of the space, in the midst of the governmental quarters. On the other hand, the space functions as a case study of permeable space where a variety of strategies are tried out; lock studies (and key manufacturing), trap door engineering, tunneling, and buildering. Along with this there are screenings, meals, readings, book printing, furniture making, dance practice and performance, theater plays, presentations of all kinds. There's also a small library. I've handed out at least 100 keys for people to have access to the space, and from these an unknown number of duplications have been made. I've no idea how many keys are circulating at this point, or how many people are using the space. I find that to be a healthy condition for a study space, in terms of unpredictability and random encounters. Every once in a while the locks are changed by the legal owners,

Fig. 4. Reference library. I open a book and read: “For Blanqui the barricade and the mouse-hole were complementary elements employed for the protection of self-governing urban enclaves. This was achieved by a complete inversion of the urban syntax. Elements of movement - paving stones and carriages - turned into elements of stasis (barricades), while the existing elements of stasis - walls - became routes.” (Weizman, 2007)

and so we run classes for manufacturing new fitting keys, whereafter they're put in circulation. It's part of the field study going on at the An-A, dealing with contested space and applied praxis. For each new lock that has been installed there has also been a workshop to fit the space with another camouflaged trapdoor entrance. Bit by bit, it has transformed into a "holey space".

> LABELLE: In this volume of the Party Studies series, we're interested to think about secrecy, underground activities, and clandestine practices, and how these often support people coming together in ways that are mostly at odds with established structures – how utopian margins, as you suggest, become grounds for autonomous communalization. I'm wondering about relationships that emerge from those margins, friendships and alliances, a social fabric for instance. Have you found collaborators, partners, cohorts there in the margins? Is there a social fabric surrounding and supporting your praxis? I'm also wondering in what ways utopian margins, and your own activities, relate to the idea of the commons? Is there a relationship to commoning practices? Or maybe we should think more about the undercommons here?

KRAFT: It's almost like the secretive has become a precondition for a sustainable commons. Secretive in the sense of rendering the common praxis out of reach for expropriation. In times of "creative urbanism" bottom-up efforts are quickly co-opted as resources and assets for economic growth; transformation through gentrification. It's a deadening experience when critical efforts end up counter-productive; with displacement and yuppification. A classic Marxist observation of alienation between the worker and the product, only that the factory is replaced with the so-called creative city. The city as a growth machine, as Harvey

Molotch put it. I find the Undercommons to be a very exciting concept, as it recognizes this exploitation and expropriation as a systemic sabotage of the commons.

What I've experienced with the An-A is that there's a common urge to escape the current urban condition – the growth machine – and that this space has the possibility of providing a sense of collective interim asylum. A temporary autonomous zone for reimagining and reassembling belief and skills in critical creative praxis.

LABELLE: The urban geographer Cecilie Sachs Olsen also examines the neoliberal city, as a pervasive model that lends to a general ideology of growth and progress. In contrast, she follows ideas and practices of degrowth as a potential antidote or counter-narrative. Degrowth, also slow life, and ideas of the right to be lazy, seem to work at fostering other possibilities, other approaches to urban planning. I also find a key component of this is Time – creating such autonomous spaces or zones needs time; they also bring us into other durations, slow durations possibly, cyclical time rather than linear, or maybe even forms of undercommon or secret time. How does time function in your praxis? What sense of temporality emerges at the An-A? If we can speak of "holey space", is there also "holey time"?

KRAFT: As I mentioned earlier, the praxis I undertake is very process driven. It's often spanning periods of years, even decades. Not only is it process driven but also concerns contested space. There's the continuous informal negotiation about claiming, losing and reclaiming space, but also tactics, tools, memories. Attached to that there's an ethics of maintenance and care, about

figuring out methods of regaining access. In that sense it functions as a wedge or a leverage for critical imagination to re-enter. What I'm trying to get at is that time is a crucial part in the undertakings I mention. Staying with the trouble is a way of refusing to produce from scratch and instead use it as a playful challenge to remain at site, to demand the impossible and to refuse acceleration of time. It's a kind of ghostly way of bending time that makes me think of Donna Haraway's statement about staying with the trouble and staying still with technology. There's a refusal of pre-conditioned time, its instruments and its murky myth of progress and a refusal of the systemic deregulation of time, in terms of working hours, for the profit of maximizing the labor economy. You could also insert what Mark Fisher referred to as "atemporality". A splitting position where time is collapsing and accelerating in parallell, the ever-increasing speed of communicative capitalism and the slowing, retarded time of culture. Bending this state of "atemporality" could be what you aim at with "holey time"? To reclaim imagination and to redistribute time towards the everyday life, away from the striated capitalist deregulation of time and away from the cyclical reproduction of culture's recent past. I understand the metaphor of holey-ness relating to the subterranean and the clandestine. The underground as an uncontrollable reality, loopholed and trapdoored.

LABELLE: I'm struck by this notion of an ethics of maintenance, which I do see within your activities and ways of approaching the city and its spaces. Rather than a production that tries to stand out within the ongoing machinery of enterprise, you adopt the already existing, often places that are in ruins, underground, or closed off from broader public use. In moving in, you then take care, often refurbishing, repairing or repurposing the place, which includes a great deal of craftmanship. So there is a deep engagement with materiality and the handling of things (which does take time) – and maybe a relation to the "feminization of labor" (in terms of an emphasis on social reproduction over production, craft over enterprise)? What is your connection to craft and craftmanship?

KRAFT: I grew up being wholeheartedly into graffiti writing throughout the 90s, something which has a had a tremendous influence on my practice ever since. Whether spatial, social or material, it follows a certain methodology – that of reusing, permutating, and repurposing existing structures. At that time, markers for tagging were manufactured from old deodorants, chalk-board erasers and what not (Kraft). Ink was also widely experimented with; boiled, pigmented, mixed with automobile break fluids – whatever that could possibly make your mark survive the cleaning buff. Spray nozzles were informally collected from whatever shop carried some kind of pressurized cans; starch spray, bug repellents, toilet refreshers. Again – anything that you could get your hands on, which would modify the paint spurt to a satisfying dimension and help you perform the aesthetics and speed of your shoe-string-budget-craft. Creativity came from limitations; in relation to time, space and material needs. Since then, graffiti culture has come to share the same destiny as most other subcultures, that of complete commodification. The DIY-engineering maker culture has been replaced by an urban art industry, selling branded and over-priced consumables.

Returning to the concept of degrowth, it wasn't articulated as the objective when writing graffiti, but when looking at that early methodology there's surely an ability and political agency embedded within; a critical craft. The increased criminalization of graffiti writing could be argued to have had a radicalizing effect on the practitioners, repositioning them from subculture to a praxis of counterculture. This countercultural craft and positionality is still essential to my practice; to remain autonomous and to be able to manufacture instruments for access, furniture for habitation, means of communication or whatever else that might be needed to make it happen. I surely follow the logic that I picked up as a youngster; the take-what-you-find/use-what-you-get-mentality. By the way, that shoe string budget is also indeed still my prevailing condition. Regarding the feminization of labor, I do consider that there's a clear ethics of care and maintenance present in what I make. When a social structure is set up and offered for a wider community, let's call it an undercommons, it's very rare that it maintains itself. There has to be an informal janitor of sorts, a role that I have come to appreciate. It's clear that this differs from the culture of graffiti writing, being impregnated with a very masculine identity, like a radical urban successor of the flaneur and the authority of the male gaze. The masculinity within graffiti culture was always very uncomfortable for me, and it still is. A holey, retracted, invisible position is indeed more fulfilling.

References:

Gordon, Avery F. *Letters from the Utopian Margins - The Hawthorne Archive*. New York: Fordham University Press, 2018: VIII.

Kraft, Adam. *King Size - a Project About Tags, DIY-craft & Subcultural Globalization* (2004): 6.

Fig. 5 (see pages 58 - 59): An_Akademie, Berlin, 2020.

Fig. 6 (above): An_Akademie, Berlin, 2020.

MIERCOLES 15 DE JUNIO DE 2016
(GUSTAVO COSTA + HENRIQUE FERNANDES + JOSE ALBERTO GOMES + RICARDO JACINTO, PORTO, SELF-MADE INSTRUMENTS + DIFUSIÓN, NUEVA ELECTRO-ACÚSTICA, WWW.SONOSCOPIA.PT/EN/PROJECTS/PHONOPTICON)
(LEIPZIG, SAXOTENOR + ELECTRONICA, MINIMAL DRONE, WWW.SEBASTIEN BRACHE.COM)
(TRIO)
(BILBO, SAXOS + TROMPETA + PERCUSIÓN, IMPROVISACIÓN REPENTINA, WWW.IBONRG.NET + WWW.REPENTINORECORDS.TUMBLR.COM)
SERÁ EN:
CLUB LE LARRASKITO (CARRETERA REKALDE-LARRASKITU 33, 4º)
MIERCOLES 15 DE JUNIO DE 2016
A LAS 21:00 00H (ABRIMOS PUERTAS A LAS 20:00)
ENTRADA POR 5 €

Le Larraskito Kluba

VÍCTOR AGUADO
AND RAMÓN DEL BUEY

For Miguel A. García

There's no clear access. It is a kind of industrial park, though one that's connected to the city. Streets with erratic numbering, uneven pavement, an irregular monotony of buildings made out of bricks and concrete (mostly concrete). There are doors without locks, which neither invite nor deny passage. On the wall there is a broken buzzer with names, some legible and other illegible, because they are effaced, burnt or crossed out. As you step past this threshold, there are some hints that the building is semi-inhabited. Bags, a doormat, a broken signboard, the remains of occasional and recent trash. The walls are chipped off, scribbled in some places, and their tint is gray and green-hued. There is a staircase that rises in a square-shaped spiral and envelopes a vacuum column which could fit the size of a freight elevator or an elevator of large proportions. The space, at first glance, seems designed for the transit of voluminous objects: like that ripped couch in Köpi's patio where, in silver lettering, somebody had indited: "every reality is an opinion." We start up the stairs, not knowing which floor we are going to. The different levels have doors but not all give the impression of being in current use. We

Fig. 1 Pau Mangrané, 16/6/2016

search for a sign or beckcall somewhere, and after walking up for three or four minutes we get to the place. There is no ceremony of arrival, we just walk into a narrow corridor with a hanging piece of cloth. The hall is chaotic and there are two people sitting around, talking. We drop our coats there, piled up among the backpacks, wool scarves and other winter apparel. Somebody approaches and we produce 5 euros – the money raised will go to the people playing tonight. We scan the immense diaphanous space, contiguous to other rooms. There is a kitchen with a fridge, filled with beer, and a bathroom at the back. There is a room without a wall – the stage. We locate Miguel and discuss ways of helping Luis set up his entanglement of cables. The most hypnotic element is the hole in the partition at the back of the room. The moon twinkles over the roofs of Bilbao and the possibility of falling is right there. There's a draft because it has rained or it will, but it doesn't feel cold and everybody is beaming.

The first sounds begin with the staging of an unexpected disappearance. They don't manage to articulate themselves, perhaps because they break off too abruptly and soon, or maybe because they formulate a disruptive structure from the get-go, and also raise the question of how to listen to things in ways that were not anticipated. Street sounds slip in through the windows: the tinkle of a lamppost, a drunkard yelling in the distance, the bleating of a bike driving by. Inside, there's the sound of beers being cracked open, an ill-timed whisper which falls on beat. There is a bee trapped in the hollow of the false ceiling and its sound reverberates through the whole room, packed as it is full of people. The breach in the music's continuum was keenly felt, as is its return, much more intense now, though it comes without a change after a few second's lapse. The act of listening intensifies around the edges of the breach and distends in the loudest parts and in the quietest. It is a listening that does not dwell on deliberate contrasts, but precisely in the thresholds of said contrasts.

One becomes aware of this as the performance advances and the disruptive structure smoothes along a series of sparkling, heavy, continuous sounds, which barely change – or, rather, it is the continuum between sparkle and heaviness which changes ever so faintly as the minutes pass. A series of closely-watched breaches ensue; the holes, cracks, and ruptures are no longer exceptional, sporadic, sparkling, but are organically drawn into the continuity of sound. In a word: there is no return, a different mode of listening is required. There come dry and sharp movements, afterwards. An interruption of sufficiently extended proportions determines our listening expectations for the rest of the night. Soft and circular movements, later on. Too long an interruption, some moments later. Again, dry and sharp movements. The performance ends by way of omission, a kind of aposiopesis, or ellipsis, that is, an action that deliberately suspends the music and leaves it unfinished.

Larraskito was many things. It is interesting to talk about those things now that it is all over. The degree of freedom is suddenly greater. The possibility of error is also greater – but it doesn't matter. From the outset, Larraskito was a workshop for artists located in Rekalde, Bilbao, Euskadi, founded by the musician Miguel A. García and the artist Elena Aitzkoa, which also operated as an informal organization and a place of gathering for a community of artists who were occupying the interstitial space of ellipses. The point was to rethink the modes of working, rethink how to establish a new ground for artistic collaboration (or rather, living together, for the idea of "collaboration" turns the experience of contact into a mere strategy of production), and this entailed an inquiry about what are we when we collaborate and what are the limits – from the outside – of artistic production. Larraskito began its semi-public work in August 2008 as a netlabel of experimental music. The community would grow

SÁBADO 13-8-20
FIESTA DE PRESENTACIO
DEL LIBRO-CD
ZARATAFEST BOOK
EN CLUB
LARRASKIT
APARTIR DE LAS
CARRETERA REKALDE-LARRASKITU 33, 4°

LARRAITZ TORRES INICIO
LARRAITZ TORRES INICIO
FUNCIONA EN TU SANGRE
SANDRA CUESTA AHORA
COLOMBINAS
SANDRA CUESTA AHORA, FUNCIONA EN TU SANGRE
CONCIERTO ACTUACIÓN DE IMAGEN Y
SONIDO-INSTALACIÓN
KONTZERTU IRUDI ETA SOINU
EMANALDI-INSTALAZIOA
CLUB LE LARRASKITO
(Carretera Rekalde-Larraskitu 33, 4°, Bilbao)
EL SÁBADO 26 DE JULIO DE 2011 / 2011KO UTZAILAREN 16AN, LARUNBATA
21:00h
entrada / sarrera 5 €

Fig. 2 Elena Aitzkoa, 13/8/2016

Fig. 3 Estanis Comella, 26/07/2011

Fig. 4 Elena Aitzkoa, 8/5/2018

DESTRUCTION DES ANIMAUX NUISIBLES
UN PROYECTO DE: MIGUEL A. GARCÍA
MARTA SAINZ
ENRIQUE ZACCAGNINI
SÁBADO 16/04/16 en
CLUB LE LARRASKITO
(carretera Rekalde-Larraskitu 33, 7º, BILBAO)
PRESENTAN EN DIRECTO SU NUEVO DISCO!

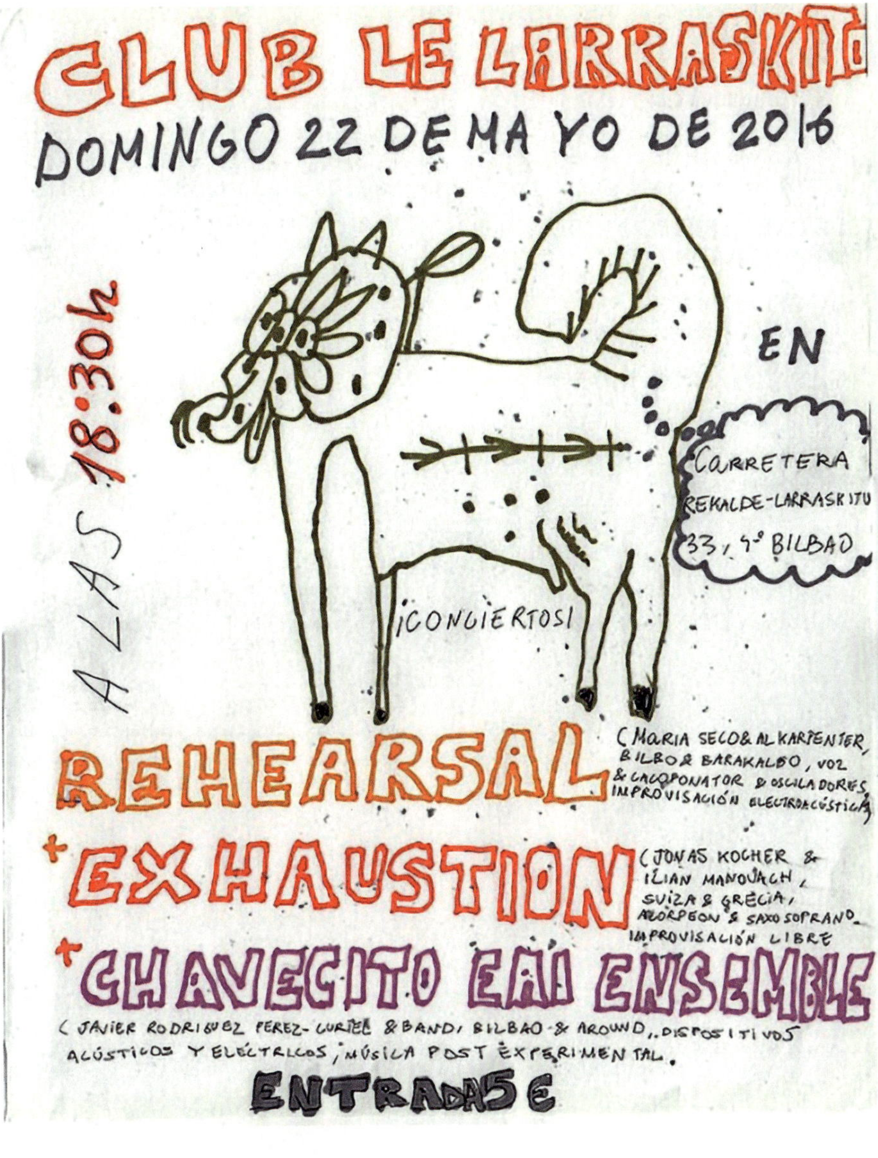

Fig. 5 Elena Aitzkoa, 16/4/2016

Fig. 6 Elena Aitzkoa, 22/5/2016

CARTEL 101!!!!!! TODOS LOS CARTELES EN: https://larraskitok100kartel.tumblr.com/

LE LARRASKITO KLUBA
otsailaren 2an / 2 de febrero

L'OCELLE MARE .
Ribérac-Alpedrete. Banjo et objects.

GARAZI GOROSTIAGA
Bilbo. Ambient-drone.

JON MANTXI plays JOHN CAGE "One7"
NY-Zumaia.

+

AFARI BEREZIA / CENA ESPECIAL
MAYI TA OIER, OHSAWAREN LAGUNAK

20:00 - 5 €
Errekalde-Larraskitu errepidea 33, 4. Bilbo.

http://clublelarraskito.tumblr.com/

LE LARRASKITO KLUBA

ELEKTRONIKA TAILERRA

ATTACK DELAY WORKSHOP

2019ko urtarrilaren 26a

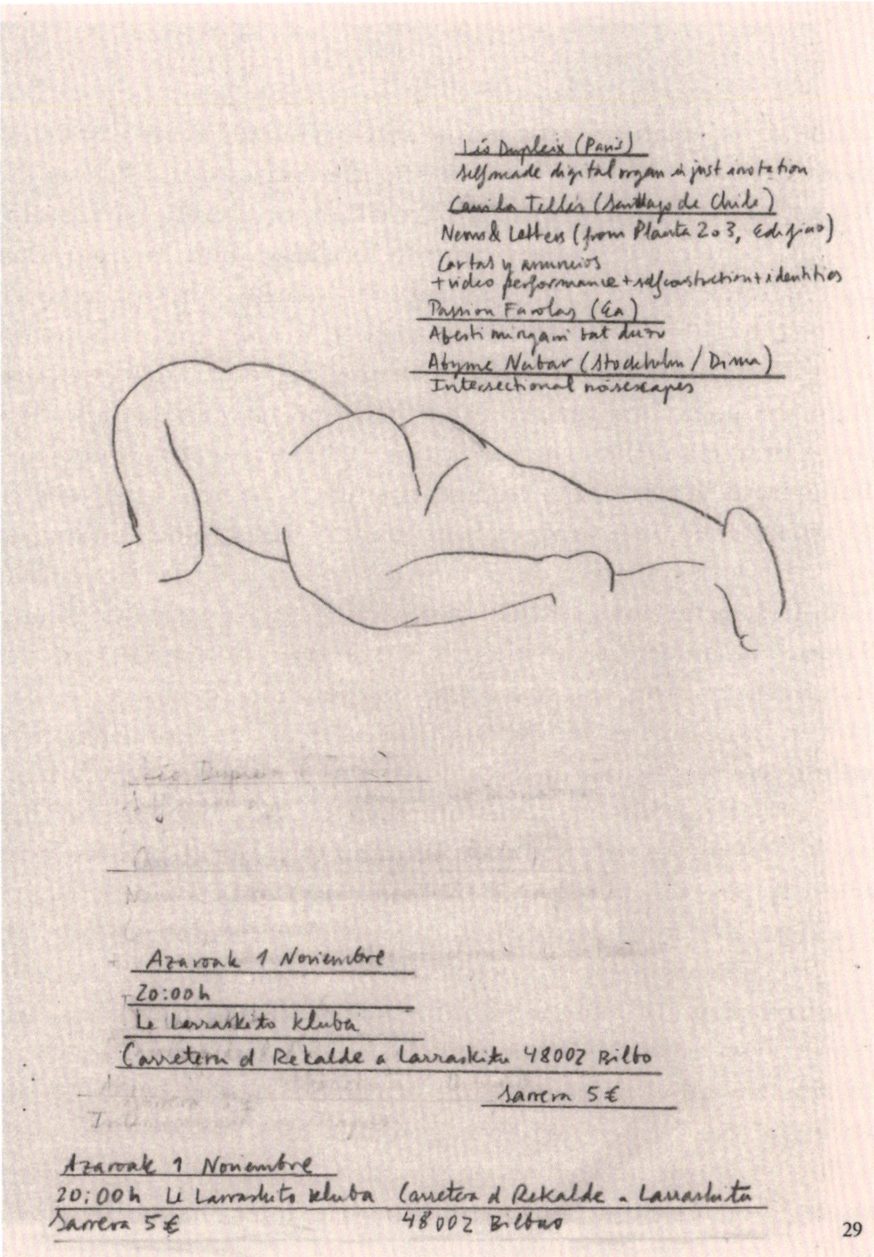

Fig. 7 Raúl Domínguez & Elena Aitzkoa, 2/2/2017

Fig. 8 Terri Florido, 26/1/2019

Fig. 9 Olatz Otalora, 1/11/2019

afterwards, around a program of self-organized events and clandestine parties in that space (under the guises of Le Larraskito Kluba, Club Le Larraskito, L'Larraskito, or simply Larraskito), a space which owed everything to listening, but, in a paradoxical manner, didn't owe anything to it, because the space bored holes into the act of listening, cracked it open and chopped it up, shared and collectivized it. The musical results mattered less than the behaviors toward the music and toward one another; more important than the resolutions were the methodology and behavioral intentions, which still endure. Larraskito closed in February 2020, like so many other things. The project did not set out with an expiration date, but this does not mean that things end. It does not mean either that some things do not last longer. There was no desire for historical preservation: Larraskito was not an institution, the space was not pervaded by a structure of power, nor did it thrive through the kind of dangerous postures conducive to visual asepsis and discursive elegance which institutional alienation has accustomed us to. The compensatory balance between excess and concealment was not associated with identity politics, but the desire and representation of the community – unapologetically heterogeneous in its makeup.

The next performance starts rather quietly, with soft and rhythmic sounds, like interferences or residual noises from electronic devices, which – one gets the impression – are there to interrupt the quiet passages. But no: a commotion of voices bursts through, barely keeping to the simple and monotonous beat; a flow of words on the edges of understanding, which conveys something more than a particular impression or meaning; multiplying lyrics spread across several voices, offbeat between themselves and with the electronic rhythm, which reveals the disappointment of our listening expectations, which in its turn brings indetermination to the results of what is being listened to. Some segments in the sonic discourse seem damaged, fatally blown up.

This translates into voids, incoherences, more holes – yet of a different nature from what came before: these new holes do not bring up to mind a vision of edges or its relationship to the whole, but the relationship between themselves. From here onwards, one no longer wonders about the form of the disruptive structure and how the voids affect the whole sonic discourse, moving on to more phenomenological questions: how do we perceive the relationship between interruption and continuity, between holes and fullness, between the myriad boycotts and the one goal? In the undoing of certain sounds, voices or actions, which delay their advance, forward their thrust, or fall in omission or intensity, what is the logic that steers the direction of listening toward certain sounds? In what way does this discriminate against other sounds? How does this shape our listening expectations not so much with regards to their relationship to the whole, but to the relationship between themselves? Thinking about the apparent conditions of the undoing of these sounds, as we do now, calls for an acoustic ecology, one that would contemplate all sounds as being articulated across different scales, perceptively incompatible between themselves but structurally interconnected. Because all the elements that form an ecosystem are important: each gesture, each person, each collective, each event, each exhibition, each performance, etc. All these things must be preserved to make visible that there is always a story behind, and that this story is composed of people, composed of moments, of feelings and emotions. Not all of them are happy ones. And that's OK.

NOTE: The documentary material that remains of Larraskito is very fragile, because it is the document of a moment. Every possibility of publication, of extending its life past this moment, would be incoherent. All that remains are some DIY photographs, some audio and video recordings, and the ephemera that accompanied the events that were convened clandestinely – materials which were not thought to be history, and were at times best suited to disappear. However, some of those ephemera appear in these pages: the first paragraph speaks of the instants prior to a performance by Luis Alvarado (from Buh Records), the second to a performance by Miguel A. García (aka Xedh), and the fourth to a performance by Elbis Rever (Alba Burgos and Natalia Vegas); there are, moreover, scattered mentions to some of Martí Manen's reflections on the lifespan of independent spaces.

LE
LARRASKITO
KLUBA
23.10.17 20:00
DR NEXUS
SURREALISM·INDUSTRIAL·NOISE
BERLIN
KAKOFUNK REMINISCENCIA
BILBO...
HACERSE LA SUECO 2002
JOLIE I & MYRIAM RZM
MIXERS·CUERPOS·CD'S·FX·FEEDBACK
BIZKAIA / STOCKHOL
F.E.O.
CARRETERA LARRASKITU 33 4ºPISO

Fig. 10 Markos Parreño, 23/10/2017

Fig. 11 Elena Aitzkoa, 11/8/2017

Repurposing unpurposeness of tambay

DAYANG YRAOLA

I write this article responding to the paths of inquiry this volume of the Party Studies series is focused – these pertain to the questions of *subcultural expression, alternative communal life*, and clandestinity as articulated in the introduction.[1] My own interest is to engage these questions by proposing to examine *tambay*. In particular, I posit that what makes tambay an important contribution to investigating these issues is the way in which it generates an ambiguous form of social gathering often in parallel to dominant structures. For this reason, tambay can also be appreciated as a platform suited to artistic actions and creative research because it carries the potentiality of subcultural and alternative communal life as part of a general attitude. Throughout its history, tambay is an undesired situation. Over the years, however, it has become a dissident platform, where its reshaping allows another form that betrays its original essence of *unpurposeness* – it may be reshaped, and it can reshape, which makes it an extremely relevant attitude for artistic actions and projects informed by social questions.

1 "In what ways does the underground operate as a key imaginary for subcultural expression? How does secrecy lend to manifestations of partying and the drive or necessity of alternative communal life? Is clandestinity, and gestures of exit, necessary for working against a given social order?"

ETYMOLOGY

Tambay is a Filipino term which generally means *hang out*. Such as "Tara, tambay tayo!", which could be translated as "Come, let's hang out!." Its original form is "istambay," which is a Filipino-adapted term from the English idiom "to stand by," which means chronologically it may have entered the Filipino language around the late 1890s to early 1900s when the American Empire took over Spain's colonial dominance in the archipelago (Batan, 2012). Another claim is that it only entered the Philippine languages seven decades ago, around the Second World War (Salazar, 2019). Whatever the case, what is constant is that it is a term borrowed from American English. Geographically, however, it is more difficult to pinpoint where exactly it landed, as major languages in the Philippines (Tagalog, Ilocano, Bisaya) all use *istambay* to the present day. [2]

There is a universal understanding in Filipino language that tambay and istambay are the same words Adding the infix -um- makes the past tense *tumambay;* adding the infix -ta-, *tatambay*, makes the future tense; and adding the infix -um- and -ta-, *tumatambay*, makes the present tense. All of which means to *hang out or loiter*. When suffix -an is added, *tambayan*, this now is the place of hanging out.

Tambay may also directly refer to a person or the person who hangs out with an extended characteristic of not having anything better to do. This may be gleaned from the entries of Filipino dictionaries and the work of sociologists, noting that a tambay is as follows: a person who does not work and who usually hangs out on the street (Almario, 2001); more likely young, hanging-out on street-corners (Jocano, 1969; Margold, 1995); bum, which has traditionally been applied to lower class men indulging in vices despite lack of formal income sources (Salazar, 2019); and as troubled, deficient, and delinquent (Santos, 2006). Generalizing from these then, tambay is classed (lower class), aged (youth), gendered (male), located (outside) and deemed undesirable for having nothing better to do or being without purpose.

UNPURPOSENESS

In real life, however, mere definition does not cover the full spectrum of tambay's various forms and shapes. To give an initial picture, a tambay/an may then be a store front (a sari-sari store, or a retail store usually attached to a house), a barber shops,[3] or beauty parlors or bars, restaurant, or coffeeshops (in more recent decades), where people gather to snack, drink and chat. An adult male variation would be called "inuman" or "lasingan" (drinking alcohol); an adult female variation would be called "tsimisan" (gossiping).

Filipino sociologist Clarence Batan's study on istambay as a phenomenon is drawn from this image (Batan, 2012). He proposes that it may be understood as a problem in one sense, and as a problematic on the other. In the first sense, istambay is a problem of society as it is unproductive, and may be a source of disorder, if not chaos. In the second sense, Batan proposes that one can examine the social forces that generate and shape istambay, which resonates with further scholarship mentioned below.

An additional view is that of the gathering that one sees in foreign cities where there are many Filipino Overseas Workers (OFW), such as in Hong Kong, Singapore, Taipei, among others.

2 From Paul Quiaño, a sculptor and colleague at the University of the Philippines, and a native Igorot/ Cordilleran proposed that potentially, it entered through northern part of the country (Cordillera/ Mountain Province), because in the 1900s, the Americans were looking for places to settle where the weather is cooler – which Mountain Province has. Camp John Hay, the summer home of American soldiers, can still be found in Baguio to this day. In the early decades of the 1900s too, Americans invested in mining in Benguet-Itogon, taught Ilocanos to teach English, built the first American school in Lubuagan, Kalinga, and established St. Mary's Episcopal Church.

3 This is why in the Philippines we have an expression: "kwentong barbero" (barber stories).

In this perspective, Filipinas (mostly women, because most of the OFW are domestic workers and factory workers) are gathered in parks, with their makeshift lounging furniture – cartons, mats, folding chairs or beds; entertainment gadgets – music players with loud speakers (karaoke in the 90s), portable televisions and/or DVD players, more recently mobile phones and tables; and food – mostly local Filipino food they make and share with others.

Joseph Salazar, another Filipino sociologist whose research focuses on rethinking Filipino masculinity, studied the flipside of this second view (Salazar, 2019). In his research, Salazar examines how husbands of Filipina OFW became "tambay" of malls, particularly in the 1990s when malls became the predominant preoccupation in the Philippine cities. The earlier conception then of tambay, representing undesired population/activity, in this case, contributed to creating a new identity – reinventing the meaning of Filipino masculinity, from being the "head of the family" as provider and decision maker, to one "who allows" *his* woman to contribute. This also brought tambay from outside to inside (the mall), from youth to adults, from no income to those who can/may afford that which is sold in the malls.

In all of these cases, we see that tambay is first and foremost a concept of communal life – of coming together. The subcultural and clandestinity of it lies on its being an institutionally unsanctioned gathering or social form. A "pulong" (meeting), "salo-salo" (coming together), and "pagdiriwang" (celebration), can be said to conduct the same activities as pagtambay (to hang out). These previous three, however, are institutionally sanctioned gatherings, by which I mean that they happen in the context of a socially formed togetherness – family, organization, religion, tradition, and that there is a given/ acceptable purpose – birthday, anniversary, agenda, etc.

In my view, on the one hand, not having a definite intention underscores the unpurposeness as well as imagination found in tambay. On the other hand, this is where the malleability of tambayan also lies – it is a shapeshifter, which makes it an ideal platform for artistic actions and projects.

REPURPOSING UNPURPOSENESS

More recently, as a concept tambay has made its way even further from its original context. In Philippine politics, senators and congressmen who are not contributing in their legislative sessions are called tambays. A party-list, Ang Tao Muna at Bayan (People and Country first) also called themselves TAMbay (Salazar).

I have taken such modifications as a cue for the possibility of adapting tambay for different applications, in particular for art projects I have curated over the past two decades. I find the unpurposeness of tambayan very useful particularly for creating art residencies. For example, Project Glocal is a series of flash residencies I created in 2012 – 2014. It involved bringing together artists (mostly from Asian cities – Bandung, Bangkok, Hong Kong, Jogjakarta, Kuala Lumpur, Macau, Manila, Osaka, Penang, Singapore, Taipei, Tokyo) to live together in one house with shared studio, in different cities in Asia (Manila, Penang, Taipei), for a short period of time (between 12 days to 1 month). The task of the artists was to try to live together, to engage with locals, and to see what would happen. Living together, being exposed to each other 24/7, removing the division between work and domestic, personal time, produces a type of vulnerability or intimacy from which the artists were able to draw their work. This "residency input/output" may of course be invisible and immeasurable. But it is a kind of "input" that practitioners came to agree has value. Unpurposeful gathering then does not

mean lack of productivity. It is through this project that I realized that tambay is an attitude more than a particular space or time. Importantly, unpurposeness is an attitude that allows for opportunities in which anything may or may not happen.

Moreover, I use the term unpurposeness instead of purposeless. By unpurposeness, I mean that tambayan's very purpose is to not have a purpose, whereas matters that are purposeless may run the risk of eventually be dismissed. My curatorial agenda then is not to change tambayan, rather to find use for its unpurposeness.

Inspired by the efficacy of tambayan to draw people together as manifested in my past project, I subsequently embraced this as the preferred attitude in approaching all activities that were included in a second project I curated, that of The Listening Biennial Southeast Asia Program in 2023. The programming was situated against "post pandemic anxiety," which means that it was my feeling that we were still looking at the last things we were doing before the pandemic to mark our next steps after the pandemic. We were not exactly sure where we were heading.

As an attitude, tambay invokes two keywords that practitioners in Southeast Asia have been using heavily in their art projects and scholarship prior to the pandemic – community and connection. A statement formed from initial conversations with those who later became co-presenters of The Listening Biennial states that: *We consider ourselves* (a) *community* – a *barangay*, a *kampung*, a หมู่บ้าน (muban in Thai), a 村 (cūn in Chinese; murâ in Japanese), or a *village, where the connections we made as practitioners serves as umbilical cord beyond the geopolitical borders. Our imagined community is where we live, and not simply a workplace*. In other words, consistent to tambayan, of not being informed or defined by institutional parameters, people come together not because it is their preferred genre of art or topic of discourse; instead, most of the time their presence is because their friends or family are there.

Following my research, I propose that this community of practice has porous borders which allows participants to go in and out of the community without formal restrictions; it has nodal junctures, which means the community itself is expandable; and it has a mobile core, where the center of activities, community decisions, or the movement of those involved are not determined by a single core all the time – there is no central authority over life. Each community in each city in Southeast Asia naturally has its own local configuration of these characteristics. But understanding the communities to have these characteristics helps one understand that at the marrow of this ecosystem is connection.

Connection is a relationship that is nurtured and nourished by shared participation. This may not always entirely be about and for artistic projects or activities. It could simply be coming together at a party, hanging out in a bar, commenting on each other's posts on Facebook, among others. It is about being present.

Among those that I have partnered for various projects, it is quite clear that our connections will continue beyond festivals, residencies, exhibitions, and whatnot. This has been evident throughout the programming of The Listening Biennial activities taking place through July and August of 2023. For this overall program, tambay functioned in different ways. One activity that came out of this is the listening session. People are gathered in a specific venue to listen to either live or recorded materials. It is tambay because nothing is really expected out of the listening session but to provide people an extended listening experience. In my program for The Listening Biennial, there were two types of listening sessions – one in partnership with DZUP, the official radio station of the University of the Philippines, where we commando-ed the College of Mass Communication as a tambayan for 3 days, making 6 3-hour listening sessions. I invited colleagues and friends whom I knew have collections of audio materials that a regular university student (and some faculty and staff) would not normally have in their playlist – for example, sound of the body when medically examined, stories of the Martial Law atrocities narrated by a survivor, a field recording of an indigenous chant, a wall of noise, a new music electronic composition, among others. The other form of listening session was focused on a live sound/music performance. This included a one-hour vocal chant immediately followed by another hour of *noise bombing* at the College of Fine Arts, and a 12-hour non-stop performance called *never-ending gig*, at the University Hotel during World Listening Day. As with the tambayan organized with DZUP, the live listening sessions may seem erratically programmed – not having a cohesive genre or theme. But this was an essential point, to simply be in a place where listening is possible for a given period of time.

The Sound Camp taking place in Alitaptap Artists Community was the longest of our tambay for The Listening Biennial. The Camp took place over 3-days in which a dozen artists, local and foreign, gathered in an artist village, where we listened to writings on the topic of sound and ecology, we listened to the environment, and we listened to recordings made on site by each of us. While we were able to compose a 20 minute audio work at the end of the third day, what was essential for the Camp was for us to stay in one place and interact with each other in whatever capacities and possibilities. This time of being together was also strengthened by how the group remained congenial to each other, bringing those who joined even closer from when the Camp started.

FOSTERING TOGETHERNESS

We remain steadfast in nurturing the communities on this side of the planet. We have a way of owning our ways. And, in brewing symbiotic ecologies across the region, tambayan, being purposefully unpurposeful, proves effective, as people are doing things not because they have to, but because they want to be there.

Tambay therefore is an attitude towards relationships. It is not simply gathering in a space or a location – it is each one becoming a presence for each other. It is a sense of belonging brought on or achieved by allowing oneself *to be with*. In this case, tambay is not for everybody; given a dose, on a bad day, it can be counterproductive. Those who tambay together must be aware that they may not be obligated to produce what society requires of them, but they are obligated to recognize their connections with those they tambay with.

References:

Almario, Virgilio. UP Diksiyonaryong Filipino. Quezon City: University of the Philippines, 2001.

Batan, Clarence M. "A Conceptual Exploration of the Istambay Phenomenon in the Philippines", Philippine Sociological Review (2012), Vol 60, pp.101-130.

Jocano, F. Landa. "Youth in a Changing Society: A Case Study from the Philippines." Youth and Society, (1969), 1(1): 73-89.

Margold, Jane. "Narratives of Masculinity and Traditional Migration: Filipino Workers in the Middle East." In A. Ong and MG Peletz (eds.), *Bewitching Women, Pious Men: Gender and Body Politics in Southeast Asia*. Berkeley: The University of California Press, 1995.

Salazar, Joseph T., "Rethinking Filipino Masculinities: The Case of the Cosmopolitan Tambay," Kritika Kultura 33/34 (2019/2020): 859-882, Ateneo de Manila University.

Santos, Vito. Vicassan's Pilipino-English Dictionary Abridged Edition. Manila: Anvil Publishing Inc., 2006.

Image page 78: Filipina domestic workers, Hong Kong, 1990s. Photo: Kristine Marie Reynaldo

Image page 84/85: Sound Camp, Alitaptap Artists Village, 2023. Photo: Mark Rambo Macatangay

Second Culture, Parallel Worlds

BRANDON LABELLE

I remember how important empty fields, abandoned sites, the cliffs and the beach, as well as pathways that crossed in and out of the light – how these were vital to being a teenager. Growing up in Southern California I was fortunate to be part of a group of friends whose desires and imaginations echoed my own. In short, we were generally aligned with what others termed the drop outs, the trouble makers, the dreamers – teenagers who were captured by existential literature, punk music, the golden sun, and landscapes of the night. In this situation, we found ourselves at odds with dominant patterns of the social milieu to a point where we had to search for alternative territories. We found such territories in empty fields, abandoned sites, the cliffs and the beach – *edges* – and upon obscure pathways that trailed over and through hills and back alleys. By way of drift and frustration, and a general air of rebelliousness, we mapped a hidden geography, criss-crossing the articulation of streets, connecting points of secret meeting between homes, the school with trajectories of escape; we hid things in bushes, we kept clothes in trees; we knew where the cops were and where the parents would be; and we kept to the darkness, often spending nights listening to the ocean and to each other.

The darkness in which things may find refuge
The darkness in which to imagine other worlds
The darkness in which life and love find new possibilities
undercover and out of sight
The darkness of shared listening

I describe this state of teenage struggle, one aligned with hidden geographies and night-time gathering, to consider how such qualities – of vacancy and periphery, of dark sites and whispered voices – how these afford rather urgent paths for alternative sociality – a space for a second life. It is clear that without these geographies, these sites and scenes, life would have been much less bearable or edifying. I wonder if I would have learned what it meant to be different and how to resist the push toward conformity; what it meant to nurture loving relationships outside the family home, and outside romantic narratives; and what sound and listening may help create, especially as a means of negotiation with the world around. Such lessons are radically linked to peripheries wherein identity can be sought outside a regime of dominant visibility – which captured this group of friends according to questions of skin, clothes, appearance, each read or positioned as negative expressions (how often our rather ragged appearance, expressive of a certain teenage imaginary nurtured between us and drawn from various references, was deemed troubling). To stand against such discriminations required an alternative logic, a reworking of the senses and the sensible, as well as through the sharing of angst and imagination, lyrical narrative and musical emotion, all of which found orientation through the tonalities of hidden places and the noise of being together. Within such a situation, it became necessary to formulate a practice, a rhythm of night-time gathering and meandering thoughts, and to craft a speech of and through difference, that is, a poetics of (dis)appearance.

I tell this story to situate a discourse on party studies and secrecy within a particular territory, one tensed between hidden geographies and those of industrious life; between alternative identities and the articulation of a productive appearance; and between being looked upon, watched, and a desire for the noises and songs that might obliterate all that stood over this group of friends.

The noise and the listening, the reverberant secrecy in support of new languages, affection, and that would hold us together, undercover and out of sight, forming into a type of second culture: it was here, in this unsteady yet persistent condition of (dis)appearance, guided by the blue black of night and the rhythmic ocean always there, stretching into the darkness and suggesting a beyond to what gripped us, it was here that something else became imaginable.

I. PARALLEL

What might we hear in this situation now? Do we create another type of collectivity, one also determined by listening and the figuring of new connections? By a desire to reorient ourselves through other forms of knowing? Is this not a landscape, a space, an arena of attention in which some gather, you, me, others? To attend to particular ideas, passions, as well as the whispers and the shouts of a global order always nearby, the languages that search for other meanings, and which capture our listening? Is there a territory nearby, or one to be constructed in which the disenfranchised, the hopeful, the lost and the restless gather? And which also resists my gaze?

These are questions that I carry with me, and that lead to other journeys and territories, other sites and scenes in which commonality may be built from the urgency of differences, and that may foster other types of self-determination, collectivity, and a shared belief in what is possible.

It was when visiting Prague that I discovered the traces of such a situation, and in particular, when I came to this building near the edges of the city center. The story I'm sharing leads to this place, a place far from southern California and the group of friends lost in the maze of teenage life; yet a place in which individuals would also come to gather, to escape, hide, as well as to celebrate a second community, expressive of what the philosopher Václav Benda would come to call *the parallel polis*.

Throughout the 1970s and 80s, struggles against the totalitarian system in Czechoslovakia (backed by the Soviet Union) led to the formation of illegal gatherings in which artists, musicians, writers, actors and other cultural figures tried to sustain creative and critical activity. Many had been imprisoned, others were censored or exiled. There was little room for free expression, and the possibility of openly appearing became increasingly difficult, as one could easily be criminalized, arrested. Such a condition led to attempts at resistance, as well as solidarity; to create, through desperate measures, a possible space for nurturing alternative culture and free expression. This would find bold articulation with the drafting of what came to be called Charter 77. Following the crackdown by the security police in 1976 (related to a music festival in which members of the band the Plastic People of the Universe were arrested), an intensified gathering of oppositional groups emerged, which led to the drafting of the Charter. Charter 77 is a critical denouncement of the totalitarian regime, and basis its argument on identifying the government's failure to uphold human rights it previously committed itself to in constitutional documents.

Fundamental to the Charter is the adoption of a moral position, one that was to have a lasting effect in galvanizing oppositional efforts. Václav Havel, along with Benda, would deepen this

* Photo: Site of underground music events and dissident gatherings, Prague

position through much of his writings, including his important essay *Power of the Powerless* (written in 1978). As Havel would argue, it is essential for persons within a society to find the means for living in truth.

Following the publishing of Charter 77, and the subsequent euphoria that would come to ripple through the multitude of oppositional groups and individuals, as well as harrassment by the secret police, Benda wrote *The Parallel Polis*, recognizing that the Charter, as a morally principled manifesto, needed an additional view. For Benda it became essential that such principles find a way of articulating themselves through the nurturing of proto-institutional structures. The parallel polis is envisaged as the basis for such structures. As he argues, "This strategy can be summarized in two phrases: what unifies and drives us must continue to be a sense of moral commitment and mission; and this drive should be given a place and a perspective in the creation of a parallel polis." For Benda, the parallel polis provides a guiding strategy, a positive form that might gather oppositional fervor and struggle, directing it towards creative manifestation. From education to scholarly life, from cultural expression to localized networks of care and information dissemination, the figuring of parallel structures was understood to afford critical social, political, economic alternatives.

It is worth noting that much of Benda's, and other's, occupation with fostering parallel structures was to contribute greatly to the Velvet Revolution in 1989, and the subsequent peaceful transition to democracy (with Havel becoming president along with other Charter 77 activists moving into the new government system). As Benda would pose, a parallel polis may act as a form of preparation for a society to come; it may support ways of behaving, ways of thinking and feeling, and of being together, which figure themselves outside the dictates and strictures of domination (and its system of lies as Havel would argue). Importantly, conceptualizing such a parallel situation instills a sense of hope as well, in terms of imagining otherwise as to the future – "to combat the general feeling of futility and hopelessness."

The art historian, and manager of the Plastic People of the Universe, Ivan Jirous would come to theorize these attempts through what he called "second culture." Second culture existed as a secret underground, gatherings and events in which people would come together, on the periphery or out of sight, to perform and listen together. Within this second culture, rock and psychedelic music were a central expression and reference, and Jirous himself, and others such as Havel, often related the question of resistance and freedom through musical expression – finding support through the intensities of free sound. As Jirous would come to argue, opposition finds its power through the creation of movement rather than organization.

II. LISTENING FROM BELOW

Undercover, and gathering together, a territory of survival, as well as threadbare freedom, and which I may pose as the basis for an *acoustic ecology of the oppressed*. There are two defining features I may highlight here: secrecies supported through the hidden, transient and affectionate qualities of sound and listening – the sympathetic touch of deep words, these that steal their lyrics from out of dominant narratives and fantasies of other worlds; and the disruptive intensities of noise, which may act as a reverberant weapon to give forceful energy to the hidden sphere and those that occupy its weak territories. These are perspectives that may contribute to recognizing parallel structures and second cultures as acoustic arenas, as sites and scenes whose reverberant potentialities give much to fostering a sense of communal effort. As Jirous and Havel would articulate, the musical expressions of various underground bands, such as the Plastic People of the Universe, as well as DG 307, came to act as vital forces within the dissident community. These are symbolic as well as material carriers that help narrate the promise of the coming society found in Benda's parallel polis; lyrics and sentiments, passions and rememberances, fantasies and beliefs that help cohere and mobilize collectivity, especially against the oppression of a totalitarian system that worked by way of corrupting the truth of words. As Havel poignantly argued, the uniqueness of the Soviet system was that dictatorship is no longer tied to any single person, but is perpetuated by way of a general ideology whose apparatuses pervaded society, down to the individual home. It was no longer possible to trust words and the statements of others; words were no longer tied to any form of truth, but were openly wielded as propaganda which became increasingly difficult to challenge.

Against such an ideological apparatus, the gatherings and events taking place within the second culture attempted to reclaim the narrative, not necessarily through overt political statements – for second culture was still under pressure, watched by secret police and informers; rather, musical expression and the lyrical narratives found in songs captured language for itself, threading it into a range of poetical, figurative expressions electrified by rock and psychedelia. Within the energetic movements of musical gathering, second culture could figure itself as a moment of forgetfulness, getting lost in the euphoria of music and dance – to lose oneself in a moment of feeling free. It could also take shape through finding new connections, meeting new friends, sharing information, taking support from the affectionate mingling of being together, of making something out of the misery of a system that only cared for itself and its perpetuation. Such moments and instances are also ephemeral – the reverberant intensities that sound out second culture are also fleeting, as the noise dies away and the systematic quiet of the daily routine returns. Yet, the meanings and narratives remain, stitched into the emotional fabric of the body. As Tia DeNora suggests, music becomes a psychological scaffold onto which meanings and memories are fixed, to form an ongoing structure and support for the self. One keeps the words in the muscle, to sing them again, to oneself, maybe on the tram as one goes to work, or while walking down the street – the words come back, and the rhythms figure themselves as a secret beat to how one walks, responds, positions oneself. The hidden sites and scenes of second culture were not only generative of dissident politics, they were equally material fixtures within a personal imaginary, lending ideas and feelings for what can be done, what can be said, what can be made from nothing.

These are histories and perspectives I carry with me, and which help in understanding my own memories of being a teenager. Although such histories are far from the time and place of teenage life experienced in southern California in the early 1980s, they help in understanding how hidden geographies, and the lyrics and narratives inflected by music, often give way to the freedom found in listening from below, especially as a support for countering experiences of domination. And which I also found while visiting Prague, again, and the stories others would come to tell me, particularly a story shared by a man I had met and who was active in the dissident communities in the 70s. He spoke of the secret musical events and the second culture, the bands and the places they would gather; but he also spoke of smaller, more intimate gatherings, based upon listening to illegal records smuggled in from the west. For instance, he told of how a record by the Rolling Stones became a precious object passed from hand to hand, illegal and undercover, to be played secretly in bedrooms and backrooms, for a few gathered friends who would listen, together. He spoke of this, and I started to imagine the scene: the coming together around this special object, spinning, sounding; the closing of doors, and of windows; closing, and the secrecy and the enthusiasm, and the withdrawal – back, back, under – within which some would find each other: identities shaped by the grooves that spiral inward, spinning, sounding, magnetized by an electrified sound and the lyrical enactments – *Ooh, a storm is threatening, My very life today, If I don't get some shelter, Ooh yeah I'm gonna fade away* ... and then out, outward, to gain intensity within this small shelter of shared excitement, angst, disillusion, and hope, undercover and in the dark, yet amplified: a second culture under the first. A second listening, making of the parallel polis a reverberant scene.

III. DESTITUENT

From teenagers lost in the haze of the California sun to the dissident gatherings in Prague in the 1970s, from the Angry Somoans to the Plastic People of the Universe, I'm tracing a poetics of (dis) appearance, one which draws its reverberant and rhythmic shape from the hidden geographies and parallel structures. These are sites and scenes in which secrecy and being together support each other, figuring into occluded yet poignant meanings, and which find their force and gravity by way of music. Ideas and lyrics, frustrations and noises that come to figure themselves into acts of speaking truth. Whether in the articulation of statements, verse, essay, or the undercover meanings found in gesture, or through an affectionate glance given from across a room, speaking truth may persist to shudder the order of things.

These articulations and gestures, and how they come to support the hidden sphere, find a point of reference in what Giorgio Agamben calls *the destituent*. In contrast to the notion of constituent power, as formed by way of the coming together of persons within a center of power – an act that aims to enter into the sphere of the political as defined by dominant power – the destituent is a turning away, an exiting. Importantly, through vacating or detouring from the lines that lead straight to the establishment, the destituent makes inoperative the mechanics of dominant power. It does not destroy what it opposes, rather, it figures an instant of depature, of leaving one's post. It might be to lay down on the job, or to delay the articulation of proper form, the productivity of a sovereign self; to destitute suggests a weakening of form – to tunnel under, to break-in, to make porous, so as to carve out zones of refuge.

For Agamben, the destituent invites a rethinking of the political, one that exits the traditional constructs by which power proceeds. In particular, the destituent interrupts the tyranny of form, supporting instead an ongoing proliferation of gestures. Gesture, as Agamben argues, becomes an arena by which the separations between the sovereign and the nonsovereign, between the human and the less-than-human, between form and formlessness, are brought into question, destabilized. For gesture is there, playing alongside the articulations of voice and the power of language. In short, gesture is a "means without end"; it is something that staggers any imperative to achieve a goal outside itself. Gesture, in other words, insists on the body, a relation to the body, on the vitality of breath and the living, on the intelligence of bodily expression, bringing bodies into the open; gesture comes to figure a politics that includes the body as a fundamental force of life, one that displaces the notion of "the speaking animal" central to a concept of western political life and through which sovereignty is cast over others. Against the ideological structures that make some bodies matter more than others, often shaped by histories of colonialism, of drawing lines between the cultured and the savage, Agamben works at exiting constituent modes of politics. Gesture, as the handling of things, the crafting of tools, the energy by which bodies persist, endure, in the holding of each, in the dance that enjoys itself: "What characterizes gesture is that in it nothing is being produced or acted, but rather something is being endured and supported. The gesture, in other words, opens the sphere of ethos as the more proper sphere of that which is human" (Agamben 2000: 57).

Following ideas of the destituent, and the gestures that elaborate the richness of the body, I'm led to consider other instances in which second culture figures itself; the gestures that aim at detouring dominant narratives. An example that may capture such an instant can be found in the feminist, anti-war collective Women in Black. Women in Black formed in Belgrade in 1991 in response to a culture of prejudice and militarism emerging as part of the break-up of Yugoslavia. In response, Women in Black staged silent, public demonstrations aimed at challenging the developing narrative of Serbian nationalism. Importantly, Women in Black sought to enact a form of solidarity for all those being killed in the war: to publicly mourn not only the national heroes of Serbia, but also that of enemy soldiers and civilians across the region.

In her book, *Agonistic Mourning*, Athena Athanasiou chronicles the history and activities of Women in Black. As she notes, Women in Black's weekly demonstrations taking place at the Republic Square in Belgrade employed three things: the presence of women's bodies as markers of interruption onto the patriarchal scene of war; the use of black clothing as a sign of public grief and mourning; and the implementation of silence, which, Athanasiou argues, kidnaps public space and the normative performance of political demonstration as defined through speech and collective volume. In doing so, their acts of public mourning extended sympathy beyond that of the homeland, upsetting the role of "the grieving mother" as being bound to the fallen sons of the nation. Through such a gesture, the logic of the war was provocatively challenged, forcing into public view an altogether different narrative. Here, I follow Athanasiou's arguments, which underscore how Women in Black figure a "non-sovereign agonism": " … acknowledging and enacting one's decenteredness (in both national and, more widely, subjective terms) becomes a resource for becoming implicated in collective projects of deconstituting the norms that regulate, foreclose, or impede relationality" (Athanasiou 39). Such "non-sovereign agonism," she further defines, "does not have to vitiate the ethical and political value of all self-determination. It might, however, enjoin us to reinstate self-determination as determination with the other, as an interminable and indeterminate finding of oneself with/in the other" (Athanasiou 39).

A self-determination with the other … in the making of an alternative, or rather second culture, a destituent politics that withdrawals from the script of proper performance and gestures toward other constructs, other ways of inhabiting national identity formations. These bring into play a tendency, a disposition shaped by degrading national exceptionalism; by putting their bodies in the open, against the dominant narrative of militarism, Women in Black make it possible to find a politics that is no politics, or that, as Václav Havel would argue, works against politics – a *politics against politics.*

*

From the articulation of form to the proliferation of meanings, from the dictates of the visible to the figural play of the hidden, the silent, the destituent can be thought across a range of gestures, soundings, instants, which come to search for truth beyond the languages of the sovereign and the constituent. Here, the notion of party studies may be conceptualized as a form of destituent gesture, a destituent discourse, one that aims at celebrating a movement that passes across form and formlessness, language and poetics, and that keeps within its discursive activities the material vitality of the party itself, as full of bodily sweat and the joys found in being together – *a self-determination with the other...* And which finds support by way of the darkness, the hidden geographies of places and the (dis)appearing figures often found in the shadows, that may bring the shadow into the open.

The darkness in which things may find refuge
The darkness in which to imagine other worlds
The darkness in which life and love find new possibilities undercover and out of sight
The darkness of shared listening

By way of such destituent poetics – *poetics as making inoperative the forms and formulations of linguistic ordering, as the staggering of dominant narratives* – party studies shows itself as an ongoing departure, a starting over. It is a scene, a language that keeps going; even under the decrees that would lock some down, the barbarism of a particular nationalism, or the weight of expected identity performance, the party finds its way. It knows itself as a gesture, one adept at vacating centers of power (even its own official establishments produce leaks and spills, giving way to additional parties and scenes; whether in the parking lots or back home, small gatherings arise ... proliferate). The party can be appreciated as a gesture in itself, conceptualized along the lines of a *digging in*, or a *flight*, as an exposure to others, to what is not-quite apparent but which demands expression, community, embodiment, and that figures a range of parallel worlds. As I've been concerned to suggest, such festivity underpins the hidden sphere: from the second cultures by which teenagers survive, finding their way through the sharp structures that come down on youthful bodies, to the dissident worlding of a parallel polis, which finds an energetic support through the sonic matters of music, as well as the silent manifestations that take to the center so as to interrupt dominant narratives, and what a body can do, festivity is a living refusal to accept the terms.

References:

Giorgio Agamben, "Notes on Gesture", in *Means without End: Notes on Politics*, University of Minnesota Press, 2000.

Giorgio Agamben, "What is a Destituent Power?" *Environment and Planning D: Society and Space* (2014), volume 32: 65-74.

Athena Athanasiou, *Agonistic Mourning: Political Dissidence and The Women in Black*, Edinburgh University Press, 2017.

Václav Benda, "The Parallel Polis", in *The Long Night of the Watchman: Essays by Václav Benda 1977-1989*, St Augustine's Press, 2017.

Tia DeNora, *Music in Everyday Life*, Cambridge University Press, 2000.
Václav Havel, "The Power of the Powerless", ME Sharpe, 1985.

Ivan Jirous, "A Report on the Third Czech Musical Revival", Second Culture Press, 2015 (originally 1975).

The Great Possession

MAURO BENAVIDEZ

Superior:
Li, that which throbs, the tweeter, the glow, the fire.

Inferior:
Ch’ien, that which creates, the bass, the opening, the sky.

Kephra the sacred beetle descends to the depths
and rises again with the sun between its jaws.

The fire at the top of the sky shines forth

EPIPHANY [1]

Late night and the sounds of the dark slipped through the windows, which had bars but no panes. In the sensibly unfurnished living room there hung a hammock. A quiet breeze and some faint portion of moonlight streamed in. From this point onwards, nobody knows with certainty how things came about. Swinging in the hammock, on the threshold of sleep, Juan Manuel Romero built images in his head: guidelines and plans were being concocted, detailed instructions, revealed – everything woven together with the precision of a master plan, of an exterior will. When the sun came up, he would execute a choreography of perfect and ruthless actions, extending throughout days, perhaps months.

For twelve years he had driven a red Jeep Willys 52. He covered the whole Atlantic coast of Colombia, transporting goods, bearing passengers – whatever was at hand. He had skirted the swamps, coursed the length of the foot of the mountains; he had met the Kogui, the Arahuaco, had visited the Valley, the *guajiro* desert with its *wayú* shacks, the jungle on the border with Darién; he had met the palenques and smuggled goods from Maicao. At times, when he was unloading fruit at the market in Sabanalarga, old Arturo Bolívar would come out and say "sell me that car there," which he would answer with a proud smile, followed by a slow shake of his head.

It will be necessary to collect some payments, acquire several pieces of aluminum to melt – from which he'd get the 23 tweeters – barter for the bass and mid cones, have the larger box and the 23 smaller ones built, and also the piece of furniture where the remaining devices will go: two turntables, a mixer with two channels, an amplifier and an equalizer. It will be necessary to commission the banner with the name and give the painter precise instructions about the desired image. At the San Andresito in Cartagena he can finesse an *abanico Sanyo* in case the system gets overheated.

He has to jump, without vertigo. There's no place for fear or doubt. At a certain point, all personal trouble will lose importance, all of his attention will be fixed on his own system. Thus, the cycle goes on closing, with the sound technician having built everything. The piece of furniture with the speakers will show, with delicate elegance, the grains of the guaiacum wood under the varnishing, and the edges tooled with outlines of aluminum. The bigger box will be majestic, its width will have a dimension equivalent to six people standing next to each other, its height will be gauged at 2 meters. Its central paintwork will be full of details and bright colors, and, as if it were a bird of prey, with its wings completely unfolded and the claws louring over as if about to catch you in their grip, with its head lightly tilted to the left, sublime and stately, it will bear the imprint of a red hen. Towering the portrait of the colossal animal, in capital letters, it will read: "LA IMPROBABLE." That will be the name with which this blunt artifact shall be henceforth known. Each one of the twenty-three smaller black boxes which will shoulder it will have the painted image of a golden egg.

How many months will have to pass for all this to happen. How many deals, negotiations and delayed installments. How much waiting and how much impatience. How many kilometers traveled. How much carpentry, painting and electric work. All of this and much more until the evening shall finally come when, upon entering the market in Sabanalarga without cargo, old Bolívar will say "sell me that car there," and then he'll be bound to smile in resignation and nod his head yes, and settle for a price and shake hands. And all of this just to make sure that LA

1. Tale transcribed from the *Enciclopedia picotera*, written by Cecilio Rocha, which has not been published yet, because Cecilio is still writing it (by hand). It numbers thirty-six notebooks so far, of which two have been lost and three have been lent out.

Barriasnuevo/22

IMPROBABLE

IMPROBABLE has everything it needs. *Todo lo que yo trabaje, todo es para ti.*

This whole thing was pondered under the unyielding buzz of the shiftless hour, that night. And resting in the spot where at some point a body's outline could be made out, now, in its stead, and against all the laws of physics and logic, there swings on the hammock, about to burst, that immense machine, with its full equipage, proudly exhibiting the red hen with its twenty-three golden eggs, LA IMPROBABLE, waiting, little by little, for the advent of the irreversible light of dawn.

> *You are willingly mutated by intimate machines, abducted by audio into the populations of your bodies. Sound machines throw you on to the shores of the skin you're in. The supersensual cyborg experiences herself as a galaxy of audiotactile sensations. You are not censors but sensors, not aesthetes but kinaesthetes. You are sensationalists. You are the newest mutants incubated in wombspeakers. Your mother, your first sound. The bedroom, the party, the dancefloor, the rave: these are the labs where the 21st C nervous systems assemble themselves.*
>
> Kodwo Eshun, *More Brilliant Than The Sun*

NAHUI OLLIN[2]

The other day I ate the floor. I scraped my knee and have not allowed the gash to heal because I can't resist the temptation to pick the scab, again and again. Pleasurable pain. Still, the wound heals slowly, heals at the rhythm I allow it to heal. Lupita La Cigarrita of *Sonido Radio Voz* is playing today, and I want to stop by *la hermosa hortensia* before, and drink my peanut *curadito*. The way from Garibaldi to Tepito, there's one point where the shops just take over everything. You are walking under a tunnel

We live in the fifth sun, the sun of movement. In this sun things happen faster and faster, this sun is destined to wreck itself in the strength of its movement.

of awnings, which look like a patchwork quilt of different colors. You find anything you can imagine, neither authentic nor fake. The sound of the multitude, the whispers of music, sounds blending into each other – everything happening at the same time, simultaneously.

As soon as I get to the dance and they notice I am there, the voice of the *sonido* announces me. That voice has something special about it, it sounds slurred. It sounds too as if we are in a cave, though we are actually in the street. It's like crossing a threshold, and the voice makes it clearer than clear that when you get to the dance you have entered another place in another time. I dig *tibirí* type of sounds: *salsa*, *cumbia*, *guagancós*, *tropicalita*. At the center of the ring different makeshift couples come and go, and show their qualities for the dance. When you enter the ring you feel everybody's eyes; round and round again, and everything begins to turn – the eyes around you turn, and the records of *sonidero*, you turn, as the world turns, to the rhythm of the turning of everything.

El tiempo no es un río
Es ya una burbuja.
El baile.
Una onda en la burbuja.[3]

Sonido is not popular, it's marginal. It's not cultural but natural. Savage, and not civilized. But it doesn't lend itself to definition because it is always changing – what moves unendingly can't bear restraint. I recognize myself in *sonido*, in those intermediate states blurred by speed. The word *travesti* [transvestite] is substanceless to me, I prefer *transformista* [transformist], it is what describes me best. It is not about a fixed definition, neither authentic nor fake, just spinning. The voice of *sonido* over the

2 Tale signed by Derrota Beckham, published in the fanzine *Reina, volvimos de nuevo*! #18 by the imprint mitos malditos, Ciudad de México, 2007.
3 Time is not a river / it is already a bubble. / The dance. / A wave in the bubble.

music, like a patchwork quilt. Everything happening at the same time, simultaneously. The wave glides through the bubble. Time, space, movement and body, which decides the rhythm at which the wounds heal. Flavor, round and round again. Cumbia, transformative sound. Pleasurable pain.

> *What connects all things is vibration. If I understand how vibration works I can understand how all realities function. In the vibration is contained the information for all things that have been projected. I don't need to see, I only have to resound. All things have the same vibrational basis but they speak them in different ways. All things which exist are distortions of an original one. All things speak the same language in different chords.*
> *We must look for the different patterns that unify us all, the basic structures that all beings share. We are biological entities which live unseparated in time and space, aligned so that we can begin to multiply and fractalize, to create other options of ourselves.*
>
> María Isabel Rueda

KUĨGAWA[4]

... I had heard people speak of the beast, which would appear all of a sudden, formidable, dazzling, always different, throbbing, mesmerizing. Devouring the crowds, only to retch them out and disappear. Something fearsome and still whetting the morbid curiosity of facing it ...

... Its presence is an event from which there's no way back. You will always remember the spell of the first contact: with the swaying of every gesture she makes, emotions widen, and you lay enthralled, wishing nothing would change. ...

... In the sky I saw intermittent reflections of a glow that changed colors. I heard the dull and beating sound which buzzed in the distance, which seemed to come from the banks of the river Guamá. I followed it until I reached a paved road. In the pool-rooms of Celso a large group of people flickered, their bodies appeared and disappeared in hues now red, blue and green. Rippling. A strange haze hugged everything. You could hear the roaring which twinned with the deep palpitations and matched the movement of the bodies and the changes of color. I wanted to run but didn't know in what direction, I didn't know whether to go back to where I had come or to join them in the blinking spell.

I decided to approach cautiously. As I was doing this, a sensation evelopped me, a subtle agitation stirring my clothes, my body – an electric bath. I lost control, and the body was no longer something that I could understand as my own. I was flooded by the unbearable attraction of surrendering to flow with other bodies. At last I faced that awesome presence that injected in me a sensation of the forbidden, maybe sexual, perhaps more in line with what is understood as sacrifice: a willing surrender to the sacred. The beast breathed into my face and I felt blessed in its presence. ...

... I have been devoured by a savage creature. I am being digested by it right now, dissolving in its guts. In some strange way I feel its growling inside me, vibrating in my abdomen as if it had been me who had swallowed it. I know it's inconceivable, but I can look it in the eye. Its form is always different. It is an extraordinary beast, all aglow. It shines, sparkles, scintillates. Its powerful roars stun everything. You willingly surrender to this guzzling, captivated, with the irresistible determination of becoming that

4 Denaké Manorá, "Kuĩgawa, comentários de batimentos eletrônicos da Amazônia" (fragment), in: *Kupe-dyeb* (non-numbered magazine), edited by ECZO coletivo, Belém, Brasil, 2004.

other thing, of blending into all the voices of its interior, of becoming a part in the invisible relations of that complex organism. ...

... We had all been consumed, chewed, deformed. The creature had then regurgitated us, then disappeared. We turned to everydayness. We returned but had lost our bearings, inhabiting bodies that were no longer ours, threaded by an irrational bond, with the certainty of belonging to something that surpasses our individual existences. Its absence was as powerful as its presence. It doesn't matter if it sleeps, since in the silence its roaring remains latent, like a throbbing in the air, a strength that goes beyond the audible, a power where all things flow together. We will never be the same, but rather will be *in* the same, craving to be once again devoured and puked, and be once more in an inexact manner. ...

The previous pages are a mashup of found texts. These three tales stem from different Latin American soundsystem party scenes – Colombian *picó*, Mexican *sonidero*, and Brazilian *aparelhagem*. The first tale was found together with three illustrations by the artist Dairo E. Barriosnuevo Marín; it was not the case with the other two tales. One can read these pages as the textual background to the mixtape entitled *Una fiesta eterna* that *picotero* Don Alirio has created for this volume with music heard in those party scenes. The word *picotero* has a parallel with the term "disc jockey", but their referents do not entirely overlap. The anglicism "pick up" is adapted as *picó* in American Spanish to allude to the turntable, and by extension to the booth, which includes the decorated loudspeakers. Thus, *picotero* is not only the DJ but sometimes also the owner of the *picó* and who moves it from one place to another around the country. *Una fiesta eterna* has no beginning and no end. It emerges from the peripheries where time simply does not exist. Don Alirio zigzags between marginal music, sounds that forged identities that elbow their way in. A great possession in which different things abound. The mestizo tangle that resists dancing without stopping.

Don Alirio's mixtape can be found at: https://errantbodies.org/project/party-studies-vol2

Embodied Nightfarers

LUCÍA JALÓN OYARZUN

The night is a physical reality, tied to our very animal condition. No human being can survive more than eleven days without sleep. Sleep deprivation compromises our senses; our concentration and perception are altered, normal stimuli like noise or movements cause unforeseen reactions. Our own relationship to this realm puts us at risk. "Perhaps sleep is inattention to the world," wrote Maurice Blanchot in *The Space of Literature*, "but this negation of the world conserves us for the world and affirms the world. Sleep is an act of fidelity and of union. I entrust myself to the great natural rhythms, to the laws, to the stability of order. My sleep is the realization of this trust, the affirmation of this faith. It is an attachment." We need to sleep to survive, because we need to sleep to keep our imagination, creativity and action alive. This is why, when the field of biopolitical normalization functions as a false substitute for the virtual, what this in fact entails is a loss tantamount to sleep deprivation and, consequently, an impoverishment of our relationship with the real, a narrowing of our affective world. What happens if we think of the night, both physically and conceptually, as a reserve of the virtual? As a *union that affirms the world* in all of its complexities, as Blanchot would have it? An inattention capable of nurturing a much deeper attention, capable of resounding with the full reality of bodies and not only with their shifting actuality; nurturing their activity and not merely a support for their passivity. This would entail a conception of the night not only as a public natural resource, which must be defended, but as a shared production of the bodies, a composition of a shared spatiality where the virtual can breathe and actualize itself with greater freedom.

The night breeds disquiet because it stands as a constant reminder of our limited condition, and so it unsettles us – not only as individuals but as communities. A disquiet that is stressed when faced with the project of modernity and its will to submit every little detail of the real to an objective control, arranging nature into a set of available things. In *The Poetics of Space*, Gaston Bachelard wrote that "everything that shines sees," meaning that the emission of light is the expression of a power which generates a field of relationships: the emitting source of light becomes a body or *dispositif* which produces its own spatiality, encompassing, in a shared field where its power can circulate, everything that falls under its spell. It is that light, understood as reaching force, which plays a crucial role in that key process of governmentality: to make things under its control *available*. However, the blurred outlines, the ambiguous causes, the always lurking difference, bring confusion, weakening the importance of this problem to such an extent that the separation between night and day will remain one of the problems modern man will continue to obsess over.

The experience of the night for a Medieval person was defined by its necessity.[1] It was impossible to avoid, or in any meaningful way attenuate, the cycle of day and night. Against the mechanical perception of time that would soon inform the rhythms of society, time was perceived as an organic flow, and just as the seasons stood as boundaries for the different chores, duties and festivities of the year, so did the movements of the sun and the moon delineate every day. Beyond the simple absence of light, the hours of darkness had a particular atmosphere. These were certainly fearsome hours, for it was at night when monsters and ghosts walked freely; but they also announced a certain loosening of the moral, religions and political restrictions that ruled the day, thus affording a perfect opportunity for communal meetings, or candlelit study, or trysts. This ambiguity of experience was brought about by the disorienting physical experience caused by darkness[2]: at night, when our sight is curbed, obstacles become invisible and details are lost in the shadows. Our ears are also frightened by this distorting exposition. Diderot described how "la nuit dérobe les formes, donne de l'horreur aux bruits; ne fût-ce que celui d'une feuille, au fond d'une forêt, il met l'imagination en jeu."[3] With each shadow perceived, with each sound heard, or texture felt but not seen, our imagination vividly draws a danger in its origin, so that, at night, our affective map – the relationships between our body and the surrounding world – is less trustworthy, for it excites and confuses with distressing ease; it is mired by errors, making us more vulnerable. Only those who can interpret these sounds, or have written over their skin the map of their territory, can navigate the night with autonomy.

1 Jean Verdon, *La nuit au Moyen âge*, Paris, Perrin, 1993. [There is an English-language version of this text: *Night in the Middle Ages*, Notre Dame, University of Notre Dame, 2002.]

2 Alain Cabantous, *Histoire de la nuit: Europe occidentale, XVIIe-XVIIIe siècle*, Paris, Fayard, 2009. Vid. Chap. 1, Sec. 2, "Originalité d'un espace-temps".

3 "Night steals forms, gives horror to noises; even if it is nothing more than a leaf in the depth of the forest, it places the imagination in gear" (Denis Diderot, *On Art and Aesthetics: An Anthology of Diderot's Aesthetic Thought*, London and New York, Springer, p. 23.)

In the Middle Ages, the night was a different place. There was a vivid threshold with regards to the day which was composed of a vast repertory of individual and collective practices, for, as though facing an approaching storm, the city would prepare and transform itself for the encounter.[4] The curfew bell marked the beginning – the term in French *couvre-feu* indicated the hour when the bells rang so that all inhabitants would stop their work and extinguish their fires and candles (*couvrir le feu*) with the goal of preventing fires. In the cities the doors were closed, blocking out all possible connection with the outside; in some cities like Paris, private houses were closed from the outside, making it impossible to exit without the expressed permission of the official in charge, and heavy chains were laid out across streets and rivers to block the movement of people. The prerogative of guarding the deserted streets was granted to a nightwatch, and there were few isolated individuals who ever dared defy the curfew. In the middle of the night the city became an isolated bubble, and only the bells of the morning, signaling the beginning of a new day, could break it.

With the advent of modernity, we lost this distinction. Night and day begin to blend and their meanings draw closer. Between the 16th and the 18th century, the conception of night and, by extension, its experience changed radically.[5] In the words of Craig Koslofsky, many European cities experienced a process of *diurnalization*. In a movement promoted and capitalized on by the flourishing bourgeoisie, working and commercial hours were extended, delaying mealtimes, the opening of the theaters and other spaces of recreation. The new States and governments were not untouched by this transformation – there emerged a new political language which courted the senses through the staging of elaborate spectacles with fireworks and light shows, which sought to substitute religion as source of sovereign authority. Almost simultaneously, and while the night was beginning to stir with activity, a whole range of political, legal, social and religious discourses began to describe the night as a space of danger that needed to be controlled and surveyed: nocturnality becomes one of the aggravating factors of crime.[6] Hence the shared birthday of the public lighting system of Paris and that of the modern police force in 1656, which is not merely a matter of coincidence. At night, the field produced by the police needed to be *physically* visible.

"Le bois le plus funeste et le moins fréquenté est, au prix de Paris, un lieu de sûreté," wrote Nicolas Boileau in 1655.[7] Soon after, however, the nighttime atmosphere of the city was to experience a radical change, and, barely a century later, Adrian-Joseph de Valois d'Orville wrote prophetically that "le règne de la nuit va désormais finir."[8] It seemed appropriate for the Sun King to be the first European monarch to set up a lighting system in the streets of his capital, and, though many cities would soon follow its example, Paris, where that double, physical and symbolic, effect endured, was the exception rather than the rule. The lighting system not only made visible the field of operations of the police at night, submitting it to the gaze of the State, but it

4 Wolfgang Schivelbusch, *Disenchanted Night: the Industrialization of Light in the Nineteenth Century*, Berkeley, University of California Press, 1988, p. 81.

5 We are basing our description on María Rzepińska and Krystyna Malcharek's analysis in "Tenebrism in Baroque Painting and Its Ideological Background," *Artibus et Historiae*, Vol. 7, N.º 13 (1986), pp. 91-112; and on Criag Koslofsky's in *Evening's Empire: A History of the Night in Early Modern Europe*, Cambridge University Press, 2011, pp. 128-130. Darkness was not seen as a denial or absence of life, but rather a constituent element of the world, an irreplaceable part of the real and an accessory of light. If, for Medieval metaphysics, light was the first principle of life, an intellectual movement that encompassed numerous fields, from the arts to science, was radically transforming our notion of darkness. Writing about eclipses, for instance, the astronomer Johannes Kepler declared that "(their) very darkness is the eyes of the astronomers, these flaws illuminate human minds with the most precious images," while Robert Flud wrote that "darkness is the earliest beginning of all things." Moreover, this darkness was beginning to compose a new understanding of the divine. In the works of Saint John of the Cross, darkness and night appear as indispensable stages →

moreover operated – just like each lamp functioned as a symbol of the king – as a visible eye over all the inhabitants of the capital, exerting, through this device, sovereign power over each lamplit street of Paris.

The system, which started with 3.000 lamps, lit each night until 2 AM, numbered 7.000 only a century later. They were placed about twenty to thirty meters apart, on the sides of short streets and in the middle in longer ones so that, far from creating a continuous field of light, they drew a line of shining dots which the pedestrian could follow in the night, balizes in the urban landscape "[which] cast a diffuse halo, often opaque, rather than a brightness capable of rendering clear the outlines of things and people."[9] The general distribution of the territory of the city was equally uneven, so that the central neighborhoods, areas of greater activity where the nobility and the bourgeoisie resided, were favored over the outskirts, which were mainly inhabited by foreign inhabitants who had come to the city looking for work. The first lamps were glass lanterns with a candle in their interior, which hung transversally over the street. In 1769, at the request of the Lieutenant General Sartine, the Academy of Sciences established a competition, with the aim of improving the design of street lamps and optimizing costs. Thus the *réverbère* or reflecting lantern was born, which contained not a wax but an oil candle with several wicks, protected by two reflectors which collected and directed the light downwards and towards the sides. Though these new *réverbères* were received with great enthusiasm – "les feux combinés de douze cents réverbères, jettent une lumière égale, vive et durable"[10] – once the novelty faded off, the people of Paris acknowledged that "les réverbères sont mal posés. Ces masses de feu forment, comme dit Milton, des ténèbres visibles. On devrait les appliquer contre la muraille. De loin cette flamme rougeâtre blesse les yeux, de près, elle donne peu de lumière, et dessous, vous êtes dans l'obscurité."[11]

The central placement, however, did not change. While disencouraged in other cities so as to permit the free flow of traffic, it became essential in Paris, where its centrality was ladened with an emphatic symbolic nuance, underplaying whatever disturbance it could actually cause. We can understand these hanging lanterns as a curious instance of Bentham's central tower of the panopticon, which would explain, moreover, the frequent vandalism which the population inflicted upon them, and the severity of the resulting punishment. Whereas shattering a lantern in London amounted to a simple fine, in Paris, for the same offense, the criminal could end up chained or rowing in the galleys. In Paris, breaking lanterns amounted to a vindication of darkness

→ in the path toward God, and in the Protestant countries, after the Reformation, nighttime worship and clandestine practices become indispensable for many religious communities, breeding a new sensibility toward the night and demonstrating that it was not only a intellectual transformation, but a shift in everyday experience.

6 Inherent to the misgivings about the night, and drawing from the etymological correlation between night (*nox*) and damage (*nocere*), legal writings from the early modern age considered all activity carried out at night to entail a greater degree of premeditation, vid. Cabantous, *Histoire de la nuit*, Chap. 4, Sec. 2.

7 "The bleakest forest, and the least frequented, is, to the picture of Paris, a place of security" (Boileau, Satire VI, quoted in Schivelbusch, *Disenchanted Night*, p. 84.)

8 "The reign of night is henceforth ended" ("Les nouvelles lanternes," quoted in Cabantous, *Histoire de la nuit*, Chap. 7, Sec. 2.)

9 Schivelbusch, *Disenchanted Night*, p. 87. Mercier, in his *Tableau de Paris*, describes it as "une lumière pâle, vacillante, incertaine, entrecoupée d'ombres mobiles et dangereuses" ("a pale, vacillating light, uncertain and crisscrossed by shifting and dangerous shadows").

10 "… the combined fires of twelve hundred révèrbes, cast an even light, vivid and durable" (Mercier, *Tableau de Paris*, T1, LXV, Réverbères.)

11 "the révèrbes are poorly placed. These masses of fire form, like Milton would say, a visible gloom. We should attach them to the walls of the city. From far away this reddish flame hurts the eyes; from close enough, it gives little light; and under it, you find yourself in darkness." Ibid., T9, DCCVIII.

as a field of freedom and autonomy – in the darkness that governs the night, only those with an intimate knowledge of the streets, of their obstacles, the meaning of their sounds, as well as their rhythms and practices, could move freely through them. In his writings about the night in the Middle Ages, the historian Jean Verdon describes the experience of sagacious and intelligent men and women who, in the darkest of nights, were capable of navigating and moving through a world lit only by their well-versed senses. In the 18th century, the bodies of people tuned their sense to navigating in a world progressively invaded by the day – people who contemplate and comprehend, in their own flesh, the internal physics of the reach of the State's power, to then rebel, create and keep the night alive as a free potentiality of the bodies. There bursts out, in this context, a singular spatial production: clandestinity.

Though we have instances of the use of the term *clandestin* in the 14th century, *clandestinity* does not appear until the end of the 17th century. It first appears as a legal neologism to designate everything that takes place in secret, in a concealed or illicit fashion – the term has its origin in the Latin root *clam*, secret – and so, much like *night*, "naturellement suspect de fraude et de collusion."[12] Its negative definition, associated with fraud, deception, and crime will strengthen from the 18th century onwards, at a time when the practices described by the term will necessarily flourish against the expansion of the normalized field of the State and its growing legislative activity. However, these same practices are the ones that will uphold a different meaning of the term, and, presenting it as a challenge to power, they will, eventually, come to reappraise it. Reducing these forms to a simple rejection or negation of the forms of control strips them of all their richness, as they are not mere resistance, but creation. They cannot be reduced to a negation of a power exerted upon them, but rather they are a full affirmation of a power of their own, an uninterrupted production of forms of life, of imagery, desires and "thoughts about oneself and the world that are not that of the powerful and escape the grids of traditional interpretations."[13] And this is so because the political, for those multiple and unstable bodies that made up the people of Paris in the 18th century, was a constant creation, not an activity for which there are an allotted time and a set of prescribed dynamics; it was that shared breathing which pervades and gives life to the streets which expresses its power at each instant, creating events and circuits of their own where they construct their being in the world.

The clandestinity which pervades the practice of Parisian and French space in the 18th century produces a realm differentiated from everyday life – which, however, informs it – and control – with whose strategies of articulation it must engage. A realm whose richness emerges in listening closely to the virtual, that is, in the acknowledgement of the real as an expression of an inexhaustible difference and possibility. Its networks and fields of action and production only become possible when the body acknowledges the richness of the affective field in which it moves, when it operates from the assertion of its irreducibility to an abstract image or a field of absolute visibility. The clandestine body acts in full knowledge of there being more than an unique path, that affective limited field which biopolitical exception seeks to produce, to define its existence. On the contrary, its action produces a trust, conscious or unconscious, forging its own spatiality which can always further its extension and complexity, inventing other paths which enrichen its strategy of life. Consequently, and just as happens with the night, we should not

12 "… naturally suspicious of fraud and collusion" ("Clandestin," Diderot and d'Alembert's *Encyclopédie*, quoted by Michel Porret, "Les liaisons invisibles : les circonstances occultes de la clandestinité amoureuse au temps des Lumières," in *Clandestinités urbaines : Les citadins et les territoires du secret (XVIe-XXe)*, ed. Sylvie Aprile et al., Rennes, Presses universitaires de Rennes, 2008, pp. 123–134).

13 Arlette Farge, *Efusión y tormento, el relato de los cuerpos: historia del pueblo en el siglo XVIII*, Buenos Aires, Katz, 2008, p. 75.

understand the spaces of clandestinity from an optical perspective, the physical visibility or invisibility of a situation,[14] but from its affective complexity.[15] Hence, more than the field of vision created by the police's *quadrillage*, it will be the fear and distrust that the police and its network of informants are going to breed into the population which will manage to unravel spaces of rebellious creation, for this fear reduces the productivity of bodies, reduces their relations, narrows the scope of their world and renders them powerless, incapable of detecting the opportunities that the fear presents.

We cannot speak, then, of places consecrated to clandestinity, or clandestine spaces *per se* – that is, scenarios whose formal characteristics make them optimal for the unfolding of said practice (i.e. a closed space into which the gaze cannot reach), but rather of a clandestine spatial production which generates fields and circuits outside of the reach of power.[16] Between the 17th and 18th century, French literary production, closely watched by the censorship and regulations of the monarchy, will offer fascinating examples of these clandestine spatialities. During the *Ancien Régime*, for instance, there is a boom in satirical pamphlets and publications, small texts and songs which render rumors and scandals into poetical form, as well as political commentary and complaint, which circulate word to mouth in the city. No matter how hard the police tried to prosecute and trace the origin of this popular production, they managed to slide, time and again, out of their reach. There were no printing presses, or editing rooms or clandestine typists, but rather "le poème satirique surgit brusquement, se propage comme une épidémie, sans auteur ni relais. Il se lit, se chante, se recopie."[17] Its slippery nature depends to a great extent on its brevity and euphony, easy to commit to memory; their secret circulation was ensured by the facility of transmission: their repetition incorporated the memory of the multitudes. For, as Deleuze and Guattari note, "every secret is a collective agency," a composition of a shared spatiality between the different implied agents. Secret cannot be contemplated as a motionless thing, it cannot possess a stable form, but rather is a constant becoming, and, hence, a practice.

The urban medium is a privileged space for any form of clandestinity. Its destiny and complexity, as such, offer protection. The entanglement of temporalities of the city produces "interstices temporels propices aux disparitions et au double

14 Sylvie Aprile stressed this point when she explained that "en réalité, ce qui s'est dégagé c'est qu'il n'est pas certain que la clandestinité soit ce qui ne se voit pas, ce qui est caché. L'« invisibilité » est aussi affaire de perception et a ses propres échelles. La clandestinité a une dimension genrée, les femmes « invisibles » aux yeux de la loi sont les actrices anonymes de nombreux trafics et pratiques illicites. Éternelles mineures aux yeux de la justice, ce statut les préserve des poursuites bien davantage que les hommes" ("in fact, what we surmise is that it is not clear that clandestinity is that which cannot be seen, that which is concealed. "Invisibility" is a matter of perception and has its own echelons. Clandestinity has a gendered dimension, the "invisible" woman to the eyes of the law are the anonymous agents of numerous illegal exchanges and practices. Eternal minors to the eyes of the law, this status protects them, much more than me, from the prosecution of the law"). Vid. *Clandestinités urbaines*, pp. 369-372.

15 Just as Deleuze and Guattari point out in *A Thousand Plateaus*, "the secret has a privileged, but quite variable, relation to perception and the imperceptible."

16 In a model that seeks to hem in the body, to harness it and make it productive, the potentiality that, nonetheless, operates outside the range of the exception is necessarily clandestine. The potentiality, as an expression of non-politicized life, haunts us like a clandestine stowaway, stands as a remain that cannot be appropriated or communicated, "is so intimate and close at hand, if we attempt to grasp it, only impenetrable, tedious everydayness is left in our hands," as Giorgio Agamben wrote about Guy Debord and the clandestinity of private life. This differential movement which the police tried to grasp in its reports and escapes time and again, for only the acts of everydayness remain, is pure actuality, never trace of the virtual, of the constant movement between virtuality and actuality upon which difference rests.

17 "… the satirical poem makes sudden appearance, propagates like an epidemic, without author or relay. It is read, sung, and copied." (Henri Duranton, "Momus janséniste : Clandestinité religieuse et conquête de l'opinion dans le Paris du XVIIIe siècle," en *Clandestinités urbaines*, pp. 329-342.)

jeu."[18] The production of a clandestine spatiality is not the construction of a closed form, of a zone of darkness as a problem of visibility, but the production of a balance which must be reconfigured with every instantiation. To do so we need a profound knowledge of the spatiality of each implied agent, one that would reveal the city as a complex palimpsest of affinities and possibilities, and also a cunning repurposing of the limits that divide and articulate the official city between the day and the night, the public and the private, family and work, solidarity and secret, etc. Producing balance is producing a body, in this case that of complicit geography where no specific agent directs the network in solitude, but it is rather the multitudes, guided as a single mind, which shape and differentiate each instant – Deleuze and Guattari, in their pages on the secret, write that a secret society always operates like a war machine within society, one which wields furor against measure, speed against gravity, secret against the public, a potentiality against sovereignty – ; a multitude for which the night does not simply represent opacity, but rather the demand for a sensorial sharpness and stores of potentiality outside the reach of biopolitical exception.

18 "Temporal interstices prone to disappearances and double play" (See Emmanuelle Retaillaud-Bajac's introduction to *Clandestinités urbaines*, pp. 7–19).

*This text is an extract from Lucía Jalón's PhD, titled *Exception and the Rebel Body: the Political as Generator of a Minor Architecture*. The ideas of "Embodied Nightfarers" are tied to the subject of the clandestine and of the party inasmuch as they foray into the abstract field of deterritorialization, which pervades the other pieces in *Party Studies Vol. 2*. This is why these reflections appear at the end of this issue. This is also why they bear a relation of confluence with regard to the ideas of the essay "Politics of Sleep – A text for the Right to Rest" by Julia Morandeira, which closed the preceding volume of this series. (Editor's note.)

DON ALIRIO is the alterego of Carlos Mario Mojica, a barranquillero living in the city of Medellín, picotero, curator, selector, collector and musical researcher with an emphasis on the study and protection of the sounds of Latin America and the African continent. His musical selection pays homage to the neighborhood, to popular dances and to unpretentious sound systems, where devotion to a single element is professed: music.

MAURO BENAVIDEZ Do-it-yourself and piracy sympathizer. Part of my activity involves exploring possibilities in the amateur dimension, hybrid practices and non-specialized methods. This includes pointing out or tuning in to dissenting, distorted or marginal logics from which remixed narratives are proposed. Another constant is collective practice, the articulation of grupal creation processes and experiments.

NINA DRAGIČEVIĆ is a poet and a composer with a PhD in Sociology. Dragičević is the author the books *Kdo ima druge skrbi* (2014), *Slavne neznane*(2016), *Med njima je glasba* (2017), *Ljubav reče greva* (2019), *To telo, pokončno* (2021), *Kako zveni oblast* (2022), and *Ampak, kdo?* (2023). She is the recipient of the 2023 Dr. Ana Mayer Kansky Award, the 2021 Jenko Award, the 2020 Župančič Award, two 2018 Knight of Poetry Awards, and a 2018 Palma Ars Acustica finalist. Dragičević is the 2023 Werner Düttmann Fellow at the Akademie der Künste, Berlin.

RAMÓN DEL BUEY CAÑAS is a PhD candidate in the Department of Philosophy at Universidad Autónoma de Madrid, where he organizes seminars on Political Theory, Environmental Humanities and Cultural Criticism. His research is focused on the intersections between music, political economy and ecology. He is a member of the AMEE boarding team.

LUCÍA JALÓN OYARZUN is an architect and researcher. She graduated from the ETSAM School of Architecture of Madrid where she also defended her PhD "Exception and the rebel body: the political as generator of a minor architecture" (2017). She is currently Head of Research at ALICE (Atelier de la Conception de l'Espace) at EPFL, where she continues her interdisciplinary research on minor architectures around issues of secrecy and clandestinity as spatial compositions under capitalism, the effects of coded environments on the body's spatial capabilities, and maps as instruments of (dis)orientation. Her work, ranging from scientific production to cultural critique, has been published in several journals and publications.

ADAM KRAFT is a maker and researcher. The tools and refuges he constructs are integrated with and inspired by the transgressive flux of the city: where possibilities intersect and intertwine, where façades crumble and radical collective imaginaries take root and flight.

BRANDON LABELLE is an artist, writer and theorist working with sound culture, voice, and questions of agency. He develops and presents artistic projects and performances within a range of international contexts, often working collaboratively and in public. He is the author of *Acoustic Justice* (2021), *The Other Citizen* (2020), *Sonic Agency* (2018), *Lexicon of the Mouth* (2014), *Diary of an Imaginary Egyptian* (2012), *Acoustic Territories* (2010; 2019), and *Background Noise* (2006; 2015).

NAYARA LEITE (b. 1989) is a Brazilian artist and writer based in Bergen, Norway. She holds an MFA from the Bergen Art Academy and an MA in Photojournalism & Documentary Photography from the London College of Communication. Nayara works across text, performance, analogue photography, video and installation. Through autobiographical narrative, political news, letters to close friends and archival material, she produces a portrayal of the reality in which the LGBTQ+ community lives in Brazil and in Norway.

VÍCTOR AGUADO MACHUCA is an artist, researcher and curator from Madrid interested in the ways in which opacity is encoded in language and listening. His work has been exhibited at Roulette Intermedium Brooklyn, The Graduate Center of CUNY, ArtCenter/South Florida, Instituto Cervantes of Berlin, Matadero Madrid, Medialab-Prado, and other venues. He is an architect and MA in Philosophy, and the Head of the AMEE.

DAIRO E. BARRIOSNUEVO MARÍN is a Colombian painter, whose pictorial work is exclusively dedicated to recreate a space of celebration of popular culture, such as the *verbena barranquillera*, with all its particular universe, in which he highlights the *picó* as a totem of sound.

DAYANG YRAOLA (1976, Manila) is an Associate Professor at the Department of Theory, College of Fine Arts, University of the Philippines, as well as Head of the Committee on Linkages, Scholarships and Grants. She served as Curator for the University of the Philippines Fine Arts Gallery (2020–2023) and Archivist and Collections Manager at the Center for Ethnomusicology (2007–2014). As an independent curator, she founded and curated the art project series Project Glocal (2011–2015), Composite Noises (2015–2024), and the archiving/research series Sonic Manila Research (2020–2023). In 2023 she worked as a co-curator for The Listening Biennial, second edition.

Party Studies, vol. 2

Edited: Víctor Aguado, Ramón del Buey, Brandon LaBelle
Published: Errant Bodies Press, Berlin / AMEE, Madrid, 2024

ISBN: 978-3-9825585-2-3

Design: fliegende Teilchen, Berlin
Printing: druckhaus Köthen
Distribution: les presses du réel, Dijon / DAP, New York

The articles, Le Larriskto Kluba, The Great Possession and Embodied Nightfarers are translated by Manuel Antonio Castro Córdoba and Natalia Baizán de Aldecoa.

Inside cover photo: Dark Navigation Lab, Rijeka, Croatia, 2016